THE
HUMAN BEING
OF THE FUTURE

THE
HUMAN BEING
OF THE FUTURE

A (Non-Spiritual) Guide to Spirituality

DANIELE

Feed A Read
.com

Supported by
**ARTS COUNCIL
ENGLAND**

Published in 2012 by FeedARead.com Publishing
Arts Council funded

www.meetdaniele.com
Copyright © Daniele.

Typesetting by wordzworth.com

"Spirituality has no label, no frame, no shape. It is an inner desire to create harmony by expressing our uniqueness. Therefore, it leads to true freedom and with it the understanding that we have no choice but to follow the spiritual path..."

—DANIELE

CONTENTS

Acknowledgements

My sincere thanks to all the people who have helped and inspired me to write this book. My unending gratitude to those past, present and future who are working anonymously to bring the light of consciousness into our lives.

FOREWORD

I first met Daniele when he became my Pilates teacher over a decade ago, when I decided to get back on stage after an eight year hiatus.

As time evolved, I got to know him better, and came to realise that beyond being a rather exceptional Pilates teacher, Daniele was also a person who has imbibed a vast knowledge of Eastern and Western philosophy and body/mind techniques.

Beyond all that, and more importantly…he also became a dear and valued friend. One of the things we both share is a love for Japanese food, and have consequently spent many extraordinary evenings steeped in the ongoing discussion of 'life'…its meaning, madness and mystery, while he drinks a little tea and I drink copious amounts of sake.

I haven't yet reached an enlightened conclusion, but Daniele has written this rather wonderful book! If you're as intrigued by the meaning of existence as I am, I suspect you might find his knowledge as helpful, encouraging and inspiring as I do.

Kampai!

Love,

Annie Lennox

Preface: My Friend (Part One)

One day I announced to my friend, "I want to write a book".

"What's it all about?" he asked.

"It's about the things most people do not want to know. I think it would be perfect for those who can't read".

My friend smiled, "Yes that would be like releasing a musical composition called 'The Silence', where all you could hear was just that — silence. Or, writing a beautiful poem in a language only you can understand. I love the idea, but it's not very practical".

I could have pointed out that his two examples have actually already been done. But nonetheless, I understood what he meant.

"Listen," he said, "it's time to get things happening. I know you want to write a serious book and I also understand you're afraid it may not be well-received since the general public has been fed a diet of silly entertainment and superficial New Age books. Nevertheless, you should not worry. It's time for you to let go of your love for Zen Koans and go for what you believe to be the truth — without any sugar coating".

He went on to say, "I believe there are a lot of people in the world who are seriously searching for answers with the realisation that we're living in critical times and the decisions we take in the next few years are going to affect our future as a species. What I think you should do in this first book is by all means convey the seriousness and depth of what you have to say, but in a simple and straightforward manner. So Daniele, please resist the temptation to fill the book with clever mystical insights — and if you really must, keep it to the bare minimum".

I knew he was right. I have learned throughout the years to trust his judgment completely. I am lucky to have a friend like him and I sincerely hope you too will have someone like this in your life soon.

INTRODUCTION

WARNING: This book is written to neither gratify your mind nor entice your ego.

The Human Being of the Future is meant for your heart and for your inner self and to build the foundations for inner joy. This warning is for everyone but especially for those who follow superficial spiritual paths of religious beliefs, beautiful words, feel good books, seminars, Yoga techniques, mantras, meditation, New Age fantasies and so on. 99% of all of this is a waste of time when ruled by your mind rather than being inspired from your heart and inner self.

When these well-intentioned activities are ruled by the mind, it often produces the opposite effect: one who is not truly connected inwardly or able to follow a true spiritual path. This person may believe they are indeed a 'spiritual' person, somehow more special or more evolved.

All they have created is another very effective escape route from reality.

So, please do not read this book with your mind; you may not be able to finish it; your ego may not like it and unconsciously your mind may try to avoid the contents. Instead, read it with your heart. Inside all of us that something is trying to break out from the conditioning of our minds; a tiny inner voice or sensation. That is what I am writing for, and I hope it is that which is reading *The Human Being of the Future*.

I could have written a much longer book which would have explored specific details about spirituality and mystical theories about who we are as human beings, but it just would not be as effective for you. In this first book I am only introducing the basic aspects of becoming a spiritual being, because they are fundamental qualities that cannot be avoided (metaphysically speaking) if we want to reach the peak of the mountain. This path of evolution that started when humankind achieved its first glimpse of awareness is very ancient and today it is mostly unknown or forgotten. However, with the right modifications, it becomes completely relevant to today's way of life, an authentic attainable spiritual path. It begins within us — with our own body and mind.

I have read many books that meander endlessly around some philosophical point of view supplying limited or no practical application. Then there are books that do give lots of practical techniques and exercises, which most people will never be able or be bothered to do on their own; worse, they are unlikely to understand their true purpose.

Philosophical disquisition can be quite interesting and emotionally rewarding but it often remains in the realm of the mind to become pure fantasy. Now is the time for active participation in every aspect of our lives: how we think, how we communicate, how we treat our bodies, how we love, how we view humanity. Everything is interconnected and the more we become aware, the more we recognize it in our everyday actions and thoughts.

Today we have to be as realistic as possible about who we are and what we can do to create a better future for ourselves and for humankind. So when I decided to write this book I wanted it to be simple, clear and straight to the point. I hope I have been successful. From my personal experience I have discovered simplicity is key. If something cannot be explained and put into practice in a simple and clear manner, it has very little value.

I have spent most of my life studying, practising and researching various methods and traditions in order to discover the true spiritual path. I have practised and taught Psychotherapy, Hypnotherapy, Neuro-Linguistic Programming (N.L.P), Pilates, Yoga, meditation and various breathing and sound techniques. I have become familiar with the teachings of the so-called gurus from the east and west. What has become clear to me is the incredible amount of confusion and misunderstanding about spirituality. So I think it is time for a new definition of what it means to be a spiritual person.

In order to understand what spirituality is, we have to understand what it is not. (And that's pretty much everything most people believe it to be!) Spirituality has nothing to do with religions (organized or not); nor with any of the various groups and cults that follow some cool 'ancient' teaching or mystical tradition; nor with New Age fantasies and wishful thinking; nor with candles, incense, crystals, statues of Buddha, Krishna and others. It has nothing whatsoever to do with chanting mantras, reciting prayers; or practising martial arts, Yoga, meditation and so on...at least not in itself.

The reason the subtitle of this book mentions 'non spirituality' is because true spirituality is based on reality, not in the blind faith to religious gods or New Age 'angels'. Please understand, I am not questioning the existence of God one way or the other but rather our perceptions of it.

Spirituality, on the other hand, is based on the acknowledgment and understanding of the reality that actively surrounds us. Therefore, we might say spirituality is a science that cannot be separated from our ever-growing understanding of ourselves and the environment. Therefore, true spirituality is the only way forward if we want to fulfil our human potential.

So what is true spirituality and what is the difference between a spiritual person and a non-spiritual one? In a nutshell, a spiritual person uses all of their knowledge, abilities and intelligence to create harmony in every aspect of life. When they find someone with less understanding and awareness, they do everything within their powers to help and facilitate that person's growth in understanding and awareness.

A non-spiritual person does just the opposite. They use all of their abilities and intelligence to exploit and hinder the evolution of others in the pursuit of their own personal gain, even when they are not consciously aware of doing so.

That's it. It is actually very simple but I hope it will become clearer as you continue reading so by the end of the book you can apply what you have learned into daily practise.

Spirituality requires the creation of a strong inner centre and a connection and communication within us, to others and to our environment. This is what ultimately leads to the fulfilment of our human potential.

One last thing; for those of you who are not particularly concerned with 'spirituality', but are primarily interested in achieving good health, a strong and supple body, a clear and peaceful mind, as well as wanting to attract success, happiness and fulfilment in your life — well, this is exactly what I have been talking about all along! If you do not strive for these types of goals it will be difficult to move forward in your journey. The practical spiritual path incorporates all of this and more.

So, for the time being, please forget any previous concepts you may have had about spirituality but keep reading, because there is, indeed, a simple spiritual path.

CHAPTER ONE

THE MYSTERIES OF HUMAN EVOLUTION

ORIGINS

We are a very young race. On the cosmic clock we have probably been around for a couple of minutes or so! This is why I find it so baffling when experts in the realms of science, religion and philosophy try to define human nature and destiny. It is like trying to define a butterfly when still in the cocoon or a flower before it has blossomed. There are so many uncertainties we have yet to understand.

There are contrasting viewpoints about how much of our brain's capacity we use at the present time. Some think it is as low as 10% and the remaining 90% is still dormant. Others believe we are (in theory) using the full amount but we only consciously access a small percentage at a time.

We also know very little about our DNA structure. Currently, we only know what approximately 3-5% of our DNA does, the other 95-97% seems to be latent and we have no idea what its actual functions are. We also realise we are able to see only 15-20% of the matter around us; the other 80% or so, we do not know what it is or what it could possibly be.

Now, we have a minimal capacity to understand who we are and the universe we live in. We are like babies with half-open eyes having a limited view of their surroundings.

One thing is for sure, there is so much more potential that can be achieved when we are able to awaken our dormant potentials. Then, we will be able to do things that today we cannot even conceive.

PRESENT

With such a tiny vision and grasp of the reality that surrounds us, how then can we assume to know who we are, why we are here, or the complexities of human nature?

We are a very young race; we are still infants.

A baby can rely on adults to guide and protect them through the early stages of life; we do not have an older race that has been through our journey and can help us to move forward correctly, avoiding the pitfalls of the maturing stages. Or, if there is such a race, it has not yet shown itself.

The present reality is that we are infants, left to our own devices, with limited capabilities to truly understand our environment and ourselves. It is normal to feel insecure and uncertain, we have to accept it...it is what it is.

Think about it for a moment, we live in a planet in the midst of a huge solar system. It is part of an immeasurably vast universe, of which we know practically nothing. We do not know where we came from, or where we are going. A meteorite could suddenly appear from nowhere, hit our planet causing our extinction and there is absolutely nothing we can do about it. All of our dreams, hopes, and destiny wiped out in a mere instant.

Most of us do not want to contemplate these issues. They make us feel uncomfortable when we realise we are still so powerless and primitive in our evolution. We have to accept we are a race in denial and, because of our present condition; we have an inner void which we either try to ignore or fill with anything that provides us with a crumb of security; but more about that later.

FUTURE

We have a long journey in front of us. Just imagine who or what we might become when we access the other 80% of our brain's capacity and when the awakening of the other 95-97% of our DNA is achieved. Think about it right now: imagine the difference between a two-month old baby and a fully grown person, and then multiply it by 1,000, 100,000 or even by infinity.

These are our possibilities.

We have incredible potential as yet unexplored or fulfilled. Until then, it is pointless to even try o understand who we are. So from this starting point, let's try to define a little more what spirituality really is.

Spirituality is taking the responsibility to understand our abilities and limitations at this present stage of our journey and having the willingness to begin a process to awaken our latent capabilities to their fullest.

PREPARING FOR OUR JOURNEY

As a consequence, we will realise our human potential and discover our true destiny but, in order to do this, we must develop consciousness and awareness.

Lately, quite a few books have talked about the importance of 'living in the now'. 'Awareness' or 'living in the now' is a very important aspect and a fundamental requirement of the journey. Nevertheless, I feel there is quite a bit of confusion about what it really means.

First of all, we have to accept that, in the beginning, it may be very difficult to achieve such a state. We have to realise there are necessary steps which have to be taken before we can even get a glimpse of conscious awareness. There is a path that needs to be followed and it is not an intellectual one, but rather a practical one.

We often talk about freedom, and that is exactly what the spiritual path is all about — real, practical freedom.

But in order to achieve this and move forward as a species there are basic requirements we need to fulfil:

- We have to make sure our bodies are free from pollutants, harmful chemicals and artificial substances.
- We have to make sure we attain good muscle structure, alignment and flexibility in our bodies.
- Our minds have to be free from the conditioning and limitations of religious, philosophical, and environmental backgrounds. We have to let go of all the dogma and the belief systems from the past that are slowing us down.

So this is about a complete inner cleansing of body and mind to free us from the past, thus creating an inner space where future experiences and developments to take place.

I hope this does not sound too overwhelming because it is actually quite simple. All we need is the knowledge of what to do, in combination with our firm commitment to advance the evolution of our amazing potentials.

I will give you a basic step-by-step path to follow in order to achieve the ideal conditions leading to the development of the human being of the future. It is important to understand that all of the following stages are interconnected. We have to pay more attention to the first phase but, it will be necessary to consider all phases as a whole.

Chapter Two

How to Connect With Your Body

In this first book I am not going to talk about anything mystical or the awakening of latent energies in our bodies and how this can be achieved through one technique or another. This is not because I do not believe in the amazing human possibilities we possess but have yet to unveil; it simply would not make any sense to do so at this early stage.

To build a house we start with the foundation. Which is exactly what our body is — a house where our bones and muscles provide the physical structure and our minds create a positive environment to ensure a pleasant stay.

We usually have a need to make our homes comfortable, a place we enjoy and where we like to spend time. The same applies for our bodies; they have to be well built. Our skeleton and muscular structure needs to be in good alignment and balance in order for us to feel comfortable.

You will notice me using the term 'connection' often in this book because it is paramount to create a strong connection. To connect means to establish a relationship and our first relationship is with our body, so we need to understand it. We must discover the best foods to sustain it and determine the best types of exercises for its strengthening and development.

FOOD: TAKING RESPONSIBILITY

First of all we have to make sure that our colon is clean and that we eliminate our faeces daily, twice a day is even better.

If this is currently not the case, I would suggest modifying your diet and using herbs that can naturally assist you. An occasional colon cleanse is also recommended.

At this time I am not going to discuss the benefits or short-comings of one particular diet plan versus another, or about being vegetarian or vegan compared to a diet which includes animal foods. I will leave that to your own preferences. We do, however, need to take responsibility for the types of food we decide to consume. It is of the essence to experiment until we discover the specific foods which are right for us and which benefits our health. That means we should not listen to various 'experts' endorsing one particular diet or another.

Besides, most of our preferences in taste are carried over from the aliments we were fed during our childhood, but that does not mean they were the right foods for us, often quite the contrary. As adults, we need to rediscover what it is we really like and how appropriate it is for our bodies.

Spirituality means that we listen to our body reactions when we eat certain foods until we discover which ones are suitable to us...to us! Not to someone else or the latest trend. This is an important first step in taking responsibility for ourselves.

LISTENING TO OUR BODIES

It is too easy to give away our responsibility and put it into the hands of so-called experts who are usually in disagreement with one another or who are just spokesmen for a particular brand of food. It is your body and no one knows it better than you if you only take the time to listen and communicate with it.

I suggest you do this for a certain period of time. Get into the habit of listening; learn to be attentive to the signals your body gives you. When we find that a particular food does not agree with us or we can only tolerate small amounts of some foods we find so delicious, we have to act accordingly.

Begin to notice how your digestive system reacts when eating a specific substance. Does it take you a long time to digest it? Does it make you feel sleepy or hyperactive? Notice how your liver responds to certain foods or drinks. If after a greasy meal you feel a little twitching in your liver, you cannot ignore it simply because you like that type of food and have become so used to it. The same goes for how your liver reacts after alcohol consumption. Always take notice, your body is talking to you!

If you get headaches after a certain meal you have to try to understand what exactly causes the headaches rather than just taking a pill. If you ignore your body's attempt to communicate with you, you have instead given your responsibility away to the pill. This is not the behaviour of a spiritual person. A spiritual person takes responsibility.

Sometimes it is not easy to understand our bodies, mainly because no one taught us how to do it, and also because it seems too much of a hassle. If sometimes it seems too difficult, do not despair; it is actually quite easy. We just have to get used to the idea that this is the way we want to move forward in our journey. Soon, we will be pleasantly surprised to discover how easy and satisfying it is to understand and listen to our bodies.

Our body has to be our temple. Exercise and the right foods are the basis from which to achieve such a state. There are so many books about how to eat, what to eat, when to eat, but again, in reality it is quite simple. Listen and observe your body's reaction to the foods you ingest and experiment until you find out which foods are in agreement with your body.

Once again, remember it is your body, not that of your parents, children, friends or nation; yours alone. Like the other aspects of our life it is essential you take responsibility.

Maintaining Healthy Internal Organs

As we ensure all of our internal organs are healthy and functioning properly, another crucial act of taking responsibility, we must be mindful of, is what foods we put into our bodies. There are certainly a number of foods that are harmful, but it is not necessary for me to make a list of good or bad substances; trust your common sense.

Personally, I avoid foods containing additives, preservatives, artificial colourings and so on. I also avoid refined sugar (more a poison than a nutrient) and I try to eat as much unadulterated and freshly produced food as possible.

All of the additives, chemicals and hormones, etc. that are added to our foods are damaging our immune systems and internal organs. If we continue poisoning ourselves with this rubbish we will create more and more imbalance and sickness within our bodies and we will, increasingly, feel disconnected and mentally confused. We simply cannot move forward on our journey in this way. It is like filling the tank of a car with the wrong petrol.

Food is our body's energy just as petrol is for a car. We have to understand what works perfectly for our specific engine. Having eliminated all the artificial substances, some of us will discover that a vegetarian diet is ideal; others will feel better with animal foods and yet for others fruit and vegetables will be their staples. It really depends on the specific needs of our bodies.

Some may feel the need for more carbohydrates or proteins; others cannot tolerate acidic forming foods or glutens. Again, your responsibility, as a spiritual person, is to find out what works for you. Listen to your body, observe its reactions when eating certain foods and you will soon find out.

I also avoid taking any type of medicine unless it is an emergency. If you have an illness or disease, try to learn what caused it. If you need external medicinal help that is fine, in the short term, but also think about the way that particular health problem may have arisen. Try to make sure it will not happen again but, if it does, it will not be for lack of trying. This attitude will help you avoid other unnecessary and avoidable problems in the future.

Understand that this first phase is absolutely vital in order to connect with your body. Do not eat according to some religious or philosophical belief. Find out what works for you in the real world; meaning what your body likes or dislikes — your body, not your conditioned mind. What our bodies need and want is the only thing that is real, nothing else matters.

THE QUALITY, VARIETY AND QUANTITY OF FOODS

The quality, variety and quantity of the foods we eat affect our moods, thoughts and dreams. We have already talked about quality and variety. Now let me explain what I mean for quantity; it goes without saying that we should eat in moderation, but what I am referring to is the number of ingredients we use in one meal.

If you start to experiment with the amount of ingredients used in a meal, you will soon find out that less is better. Every food has its own energetic vibration that affects our moods. When you consume a meal comprising only three or four simple ingredients; for example, a spinach omelette with potatoes or carrots, or rice with beans and a salad; and then continue eating these types of meals, for several days you will notice your mind will become calmer, you will have less mood swings and enjoy a better quality of sleep.

Frequently we use too many ingredients, sometimes twenty or more in one meal. This results in a lot of different vibrational energies which may conflict depending on the food combination. This can result in an overactive mind, confusion and restlessness not only in our daily life but also during sleep and dreaming.

LIFE FORCE

Another important point to make is that we should make an effort to only eat fresh foods which still retain their life force. A fresh fruit or vegetable (not green or overripe) is at its fullest when it is vibrant and full of life energy, just like a human being who has reached their energetic peak at the end of the growing phase. This is when fruit or vegetables should be eaten in order to absorb a vibrant, healthy energy that will nourish our bodies. Seeds, nuts, sprouts, pulses and whole grains also retain the life energy we need, so basically any food that grows naturally.

Processed foods, flour products, animal and dairy foods, energetically speaking, are dead foods. They can provide the nutriments necessary for our bodies, but not the vibrant and clear energy (life force) we need.

If you are suffering from depression, start eating more foods that retain their life force and you will soon notice the difference. You do not have to believe me, just try it for a while, experiment and find out what works best for you. Some people will discover their bodies function better with animal foods, which is perfectly fine because it is the present reality. But remember, energetically speaking, it is dead food, so try to balance it with the types of fresh foods I have described.

When we start on the path of inner discovery we may soon find out we need less of anything we previously thought was necessary. This is why I cannot stress enough the importance of taking full responsibility yourself without relying on so-called 'experts'. If we are serious about living in the now, self-awareness and accountability is paramount.

Freedom is not some childish idea of being able to do whatever we want. Real freedom comes with achieving a state of health and balance in which we feel free from sickness and mental conditioning. The choice is yours, whatever you ultimately decide you want to do with your body and your life (unless it is impinging on other people's freedom) is perfectly fine. Every action has its consequences and as long as you know and are prepared to accept those consequences, you can do whatever you want.

Let me make something even clearer for those of you who want to follow this path: you do not have to deprive yourself of the things you enjoy. It just means that you have to enjoy them with awareness and responsibility. If you go out and get drunk or overeat on your favourite foods, that is also fine, as long as you are prepared for the consequences that will be happening in your body and mind.

In the long run, you may discover that a healthy body and mind and the amazing feeling derived from it are more important, so you may choose to reduce and perhaps eliminate certain habits. If you still find the pleasure of certain excesses is something you just cannot do without, that's also fine...it is your choice.

CHAPTER THREE

THE PHYSICAL BODY: CREATING A STRONG FOUNDATION

ALIGNMENT AND MUSCLE BALANCE

Connecting with our bodies involves more than taking care of its internal organs; we also have to strengthen our external structure. We need to make sure we achieve good posture, muscle structure, alignment and flexibility. In order to maintain this optimal condition we have to discover the right exercises which work for our bodies.

Imagine your body as a house. If the walls are falling down, the pipes are rusty and the electrical system faulty; until you have taken care of these basic problems, it is very difficult to focus on anything else. Our bodies have to be just like a house — solid in its foundation. Our muscles and nerves need to be strong and healthy so we can relax and focus on other aspects of our spirituality, knowing our foundation supports us. Having a well-built body is the best possible preparation for experiencing a new state of consciousness and evolutionary awakening.

EXERCISE

In order for our bodies to work harmoniously we have to make sure that, just like the frame of a house, our muscles are developed equally and are in equilibrium. It makes no sense to build major muscle groups for the purpose of satisfying some imaginary ideals of 'looking good' and at the same time forgetting other minor muscle groups, equally important, but less outwardly noticeable. This infatuation of working out with heavy weights is unnatural and unnecessary and we have to move away from it. Having bulking muscles when others are undeveloped or lack flexibility is not strength, but imbalance and very often they just slow us down.

We have to move away from this mentality and find out what type of exercise routine is best to achieve a strong, equally developed muscle structure that will support our bodies now and during our older years. Personally, I have discovered Yoga and Pilates are the best forms of exercise available. Also, martial arts when removed from excessive macho tendencies...but hey, maybe you know something I don't!

Strength is having properly formed muscles which are achieved by doing exercises using light weights, or even better, our own body weight. This will produce muscles that are long, flexible, equally developed and in alignment, thus providing us with good posture, balance, flexibility and the ability of fast movement. Besides, bulking muscles will eventually turn into flab as we grow older.

I have suggested Yoga and Pilates as an excellent form of exercise, but once again look around, experiment, be inquisitive, listen to your body and you will find what is optimal for you.

Those of you who are becoming more and more sensitive and connected to the state of their body and mind who have begun taking responsibility, will slowly realise the new feelings of clarity and awareness far outweigh any previous form of satisfaction.

TRAPPED EMOTIONS

If we want to reach the top of the mountain we have to be in the best possible condition, because this is not a mountain peak we can reach by helicopter. It has to be climbed day by day, moment by moment. Be very suspicious of anyone who offers short cuts.

Even the way we exercise has to be done with an awareness of what is happening in our body and mind, and an understanding of how it is related to emotions. We tend to store emotional states in our muscles and body structure. Many times, painful memories or negative emotional states are suppressed, because it would be too painful or uncomfortable to bring them to the surface.

In order to cope with everyday life, and be able to maintain a semblance of emotional balance, we do not access these emotional states but, nevertheless, they are there, inside of us — in our muscles, and many times they determine the way we relate to our bodies.

I have witnessed many people who carry with them the negative experiences they are trying to forget. They tend to create an excessive amount of stiffness in their bodies, they avoid stretching because unconsciously they know it will cause the release of emotional states trapped in the muscular structure.

It is an unconscious way to remain in control while being able to function and cope with the realities of everyday life. Ironically, it is not at all uncommon to manifest repressed feelings as we become more flexible.

The same people that avoid stretching are often obsessed with working out hard with weights, running or strong physical exercise. Burning energy through physical exertion allows us to feel calmer simultaneously burning away any emotional states that may make us feel uncomfortable. So, if you are angry with someone, going to the gym, or for a run, will make you feel better because you will have burnt away the negative energy (until the next time).

The understanding that our bodies need the right foods and forms of exercise has to be combined with an understanding of our minds and emotional states. I have frequently noticed that people who have a flexible body can be quite emotionally fragile, and find it difficult to control their inner emotional state. Often, when beginning some form of exercise like Yoga or Pilates, they feel good because their bodies needed to stretch and create more flexibility. Unfortunately as the body starts to become more flexible, it seems no longer able to contain the emotional imbalances that the previous state of rigidity was able to suppress.

Consequently, some begin to feel more nervous, fragile and often confused, without any idea as to why this is happening. The last thing they would imagine is this delicate state has come as a result of the very exercise their body so sorely needed.

Once again we need to take responsibility and listen to our bodies but, this time, be aware of our mental and emotional states, making sure they receive the same attention we give to our bodies. As soon as we notice some emotional imbalances, we must try to understand where they originated from, and deal with them accordingly. It is important that the health of our body and mind improve, in parallel, as they are so dependent on one another.

This is why, even though the first step of the journey begins with our bodies, we still have to be constantly aware of other aspects that influence its optimum functionality. If you have a disability or sickness, do not feel you are in a disadvantageous position. You can still take care of your nutrition and if your physical body is not supporting you as you would like, it does not matter, there are other ways to keep you on the right spiritual path like breathing techniques and the power of a focused mind. I will deal with this more deeply in *Chapter 9 – Gaining Focus and Awareness.*

BREATHING

Most of us breathe just enough to keep us alive. Breathing is very important and learning how to extend our breath as we inhale and exhale can give us so much more energy and vitality. What keeps the body in a healthy state is the flow of life energy that goes through it and breathing brings this life energy into our lungs and throughout our body.

I want to keep this very simple. The energy flow in our bodies happens freely when we breathe fully and our bodies are in a relaxed state. When we have stiffness in our bodies, whatever the cause, lack of exercise or tension created by a worrying mind, it will impede our energy flow.

Knowledge of pressure points can help, shaking the whole body every day for few minutes also helps and, of course, stretching.

By far the most effective way to guarantee a healthy flow of energy is through breathing techniques.

Very simply, learn to lengthen the amount of time you inhale and exhale, for as long as you can, while in a relaxed state. Take long, slow, deep breaths. Five seconds is fine to start with, but eventually try to extend it up to seven seconds or more. For the time being, doing this a few minutes a day will be a good start.

CHAPTER FOUR

EVIL

Evil; this is the heart of the book. I know it may seem strange, but please read on. Just as the heart regulates the function of the body, this chapter gives a much deeper meaning to everything previously written, as well as what will follow.

THE CONSEQUENCES OF OUR ACTIONS

There have been so many books written about evil, dark forces, magic, the devil and variations on this theme, I would like to present a different way to look at what evil is and how it manifests itself in our lives. First of all I will define it in one sentence and from there we can expand.

Evil is the unavoidable consequence or leftovers created by the process of evolution.

Let's keep this in mind as we proceed. To grasp the big picture, as always, we have to start with our bodies. We all know if we eat something 'spoiled' we will feel sick, probably suffer stomach pains and possibly vomit. We could say that that resulted in a negative outcome… or 'evil'. At first it may sound a bit simplistic, but this is not so.

The same happens if we eat too much of the wrong foods for our bodies; often, it will result in a feeling of discomfort, stomach pain or a headache. We have created an evil as a result of our actions. Over time, if we are lazy and fail to care for our bodies, we create imbalance, severe stiffness, back pain and so on. Consequently, we produce an evil result, rather than the possibility of a balanced well-structured body, free from aches and pains.

Neglecting our bodies and eating the wrong foods will not only affect our bodies but also our mind creating an unbalanced state. These negative conditions in our bodies and minds will keep us in a negative state in which we are not able to inwardly feel happy and in harmony. By consequence, our external actions also will not be harmonious. They will be detrimental to us and others because they are motivated by anger, bitterness, envy and so on. This will result in inner disharmony. Therefore, unless we treat our bodies properly these harsh consequences are unavoidable and will surely result in inner disharmony.

Our negative actions, words and thoughts are constantly creating negativity or evil. The vast amount of evil we experience in the world is connected with our inner states. It is important to understand that our everyday actions can have an influence on the overall amount of evil in the world. So while it goes without saying we have to cope with the big picture, we must not forget that it starts with us.

We have to understand and consider that our limited level of consciousness, in our primitive stage of evolution, has been based on the need for individual survival up to now. This has created an incredible amount of what we could describe as negativity or 'darkness'. Basically it is 'evil' only because we are still in a transitional phase between the unconscious savageness of the past and the conscious, enlightened, human being of the future.

The evil we have created so far is very real; it can be seen every day in the news. It is an overall presence in the planet, revealed in how we are relate to each other, manifested in continuing conflict between race, religion, nationality and social background. We can also see evil within the circles of our close family and friends, when our interactions are based on selfishness and suspicion.

THE CHOICE BETWEEN GOOD AND EVIL

As we increase our awareness, we better understand the significance of the ability to choose good over evil. We begin to understand what creates evil and what we can do to choose good. We also realise that those less aware create evil unconsciously and their power to create evil is limited, just like their awareness. The more aware also bear more responsibility because their power is greater when they choose to use their awareness and the abilities that come with it. It is inexcusable of them to control, manipulate and exploit others when they are conscious of what they are doing.

From a religious point of view they are the Satanists, or the black magicians; self-deluding beings who have chosen the path of selfish power to achieve their means at the expense of others. These ones create and feed the vast majority of evil in the world. Those with little awareness are just caught in this lower vibration and act accordingly, hardly able to choose for themselves.

We must become aware of the evil repercussions of our thoughts and actions, making sure we do whatever we can to reduce the amount of negative energy we create, by our still limited awareness. Fortunately, our awareness will increase steadily as we take responsibility and proceed along the path of evolution.

SELFISH LOVE

I am mentioning selfish love now because we should stop romanticizing what is actually a selfish need in order to fill an inner void since it creates so much evil in the world.

This so-called love that people often manifest towards another person is just a thinly disguised need for acceptance, security and a fear of loneliness. Often we profess our love for this person just for our 'love' to last only as long as the other person reciprocates. Should that other person fall in love with someone else, then our love changes into bitterness, anger and resentment. At the same time, somehow, we still believe we are in love with the person. How can anyone think these emotions arise from love? Would real love result in such a lower negative state of consciousness? Not at all!

In time we will find another person to love and, in so doing, we will again fill our inner void or fear of loneliness. We will defend, support and cling on to the new person we now 'love' because they are our security blanket, giving meaning to our life; a life that quite justifiably seems meaningless in our present state.

But how could it be any different when the reality is that we are new beings, with limited knowledge of ourselves? Basically, we are like small children, usually thinking only of themselves. Let's accept that this is our present state of evolution. There is no one else to blame; it is largely who we are but, at the same time, we can look at how we can effectively fill the inner void. The answer lies in achieving awareness.

I say that this is who we are 'largely' because we also possess, within us, the positive potential and capacity to create a strong inner centre which will fill the void, based on self-love distinct from selfishness. We also have the ability to truly love unconditionally and so bring light to where darkness resides reducing the unavoidable evil we created. It can be done quite easily but we have to follow the path of conscious evolution.

HAPPINESS AS A NATURAL CONSEQUENCE

Many people genuinely try to be good because they want to do their best in life and be a 'good' person. This pursuit in itself is admirable but it misses the point. Struggling to be good is an erroneous activity, it is not something you can try for, either you are or you are not.

You are in a state of imbalance because your body is unhealthy, due to the foods you eat and your physical core lacks good muscle structure and balance. Your mind is filled with negative emotions or you live your life robotically without much awareness — yes, it is likely you will struggle to overcome temptation.

When you are 'in tune', meaning your body is healthy, your organs are working properly, you have started to work on your mind, you have begun clearing the negativity of the past and you are led by your 'Higher Self'; you will not need to try to be good, it will be a natural consequence! So the real emphasis is about doing the right thing, thus avoiding the struggle and thence not creating negativity in your life.

A lot of people who are in an imbalanced state fight all the time as they try to overcome their personal challenges: their jealousy, their anger, their competition, their depression, their addictions and so on. Unfortunately they are often fighting a losing battle because it is very tough to conquer these challenges without taking care of the things discussed in this book first: the body, mind and spirit.

If you place a flower in a pot where the soil is poor and lacks nutrients, deprive it of sunlight and then fail to give it water, the flower will struggle to survive; it will be difficult for the flower to blossom. However, if you place the flower in nutrient rich soil, give it the right amount of water, and expose it to sunlight, the flower will blossom, reaching its full potential of beauty as a natural consequence.

These days much is talked about problem children and difficult teenagers. How difficult it must be for them to avoid these crazy periods in their life, if they have developed in an unhealthy family situation with parents who are not in tune. The parents are often the source of the child's problems. In these situations, the developing child is bound to experience unnecessary challenges, in order to overcome all the imbalances created during the earlier stages of their life.

The child should be like the flower in many ways. We have to give them the right foods, encourage them to keep their body strong and healthy, explain how the mind works and help them discover their own Higher Self. Essentially we should be giving them the best of what we have learned so they do not have to struggle so much to be positive, or to find happiness in life.

Remember, happiness should be a natural consequence of being a human being and being alive

CHAPTER FIVE

THE MIND

In our present state of awakened sleep, it is very difficult to be in total control of our mind. Those who have seriously tried to do it can testify that it can only be done for brief moments. In fact, most of the time we are not even aware of how our thoughts are being processed or how our random thoughts often take us on an emotional roller-coaster ride over which we have little or no control.

THE INFLUENCE OF PAST EVENTS

Oftentimes, our mind is cluttered with unwanted thoughts which are linked to emotional experiences from the past. These experiences usually have not been dealt with and have quietly debilitated us. In order to free our minds from such unwanted thoughts we need to understand that the mind is rather like a computer.

When we store a large amount of information on our computer, it can slow down the system if we do not take the time to delete old files that are no longer useful or relevant. Our 'old files' are the past events that have left a destructive mark on our lives and still influence our everyday actions. Some have left such a powerful impression on our psyche, we are likely to carry them with us for the rest of our lives.

It is difficult to control these random thoughts because we are often not aware of them. Usually one unconscious thought is triggered by a series of other unconscious thoughts. Perhaps we are busy, doing something on which we are content and focused, when a random thought pops into our mind. We then follow, almost robotically, wherever our thinking decides to take us. Soon, this first random thought meets a second random thought, spinning us in another direction where it links with yet a third random thought, and so this mechanical cycle continues.

Often these random thoughts are related to unpleasant past events or future worries. Depending on how strongly we are influenced by the situation, these toxic feelings can stay with us for quite a while and, in so doing, negatively affect our present behaviour.

This happens to many people who, unconsciously, continue through life blindly following thought patterns which are often connected with unpleasant past events. Inevitably, those old negative emotions resurface, hindering their present forward progress, to steer them in the wrong direction.

BECOMING AWARE OF OUR THOUGHT PATTERNS

During our life we tend act and react in the same way. When we allow ourselves to be led by unconscious impulses rooted in negative past experiences, we begin to create a false personality with its own set of rules and behaviours. As a result we randomly travel through life without having clear direction.

It is imperative we develop a deep awareness of our thought patterns and learn how to better control them. Rather than follow our thoughts aimlessly, we must use our will to knowingly decide what we want to think about, until we make the decision to think about something else. Once we learn how to do this, with total mental and emotional freedom, we will discover we have created a clear path toward our future.

We have already discussed the health of the body, which is relatively easy to understand and implement. A healthy mind is rather more challenging because we are dealing with emotions; every time we have a negative thought; it leads to a negative emotion. Therefore, from this point forward we must learn how to enjoy having more positive thoughts which will lead us to healthier emotions and create more harmony around us.

If we go through life carrying with us negative belief systems because of negative and sometimes traumatic past events, how do we deal with them?

Certainly there are an abundance of different kinds of therapies and mind techniques dealing with emotions. Many people spend years in treatment with varying degrees of success; personally, I would suggest keeping it simple

Our perceptions create our present reality.

We have all been through unpleasant experiences which have shaped the way we are today, but their significance lies in our perceptions. We need to learn to release any negative feelings we harbour about the people and events from our past.

Sometimes things have happened which were truly horrific; in such situations the challenge will be even greater; regardless, we have to forgive and let go. This is not only for our own benefit, but because those negative feelings and perceptions, also affect those around us.

MEMORY AND AWARENESS EXERCISE

Try this exercise right now!

It is incredibly powerful, not only for the memory but in developing your awareness. It will go a long way to preventing you from continuing to move mechanically through life:

At the end of the evening, even better if you are in bed, comfortable and relaxed, I want you to relive the day in a 2-3 minute movie.

For example, think about the first things you did when you woke up in the morning.

Perhaps you went to the bathroom, brushed your teeth and took a shower. (Really relive it). Then, maybe you got in your car to go to work and then checked your morning emails, etc. The idea is to remember everything you have done during the day until the moment you went to bed and began this exercise

This exercise is so effective is because you will begin to develop a sense of awareness of your daily actions.

> You can analyse if it was indeed a good day or bad day.
> Did you do the things you had wanted to do?
> Did you do something you wish you hadn't?
> Is life going in the direction you want it to?

It is so necessary that we develop this ability to become aware and connect because when there is no connection we can drift from month to month, often year to year, doing things we do not even enjoy just because we never took the time to stop and focus.

GETTING RID OF NEGATIVE EMOTIONS

To help you become successful in getting rid of negative emotions, this idea may help.

We have to continuously remember we are very young beings in human evolution; therefore, we are prone to make mistakes. Often we are at the mercy of lower emotions that give birth to negative, selfish behaviour. No one is bad or evil, just beings in a still primitive stage of evolution.

No matter what someone did to you in the past, it was not personal, even if it seems otherwise.

It was just an insecure, selfish, misguided and disconnected being trying to survive the only way they could.

If not you, it would have been someone else.

Before we go any further I want to point out what follows is not an intellectual disquisition. There is no technique in this chapter (or any other part of this book) where I have not had personal experience in its application. I, too, have had my share of tough times and applied the following techniques which have proved to be extremely effective. I believe you too can experience success if you have an open mind and apply them earnestly.

Believe me, I understand sometimes it may seem impossible to forgive the people who have done horrible things to us, but it can be done. Indeed, it has to be done, if we want to break the chain of negativity and reduce the evil on the planet.

With this in mind, let's do something about it.

CHAPTER SIX

FORGIVENESS

CHANGING THE PERCEPTIONS OF NEGATIVE PAST EXPERIENCES

This simple exercise should be done until you are truly free from negative past experiences:

1   Lie down in a quiet room.

    Make sure your environment is relaxing, use soft lights, candles, incense or whatever works to help you to connect inwardly.

2   Listen for a few seconds to any external sounds and sensations.

3   Bring your attention to your body and keep it there the whole time.

    If it helps, also focus on your breathing for few minutes.

4   Recall a negative or traumatic event of your past.

    You can start with a small one if you prefer and relive it like a short movie:

    For example, let's say when you were ten years old you accidentally broke something valuable in your house. When your mother entered the room she lost her temper and slapped you...hard. She then yelled things like *'You're a disaster'*, *'You are useless'*, *'You don't care'*, *'You'll never accomplish anything in your life...'*

    If you can still remember an event like this, there is a good chance it still affects your life and self-esteem today and has influenced the way you believe your mother feels about you.

    What you need to do is change the script. Staying with this particular example, now that you are an adult, imagine what your mother's life and situation may have been at the time.

5   Then add another part to the movie.

After your mother has slapped you and left you alone in the room, picture her coming back with a different attitude. The script could be something like this: *'I am so sorry I slapped you and said all of those terrible things. I've been really stressed lately, we've been having money problems and things between your father and I are not going very well...and, unfortunately I took my frustration out on you'.*

So, in the second part of the example, you begin to feel differently about your mother's behaviour, because a feeling of compassion for her would have replaced the previous feelings of her disapproval of you. In addition, the way you now think about yourself will be healthier, because the old negative feelings were based on false assumptions.

Your particular situation may be different, or it can be quite similar, but I can assure you the script you add to your past event is very close to the truth. The key is to relive it, in your mind, until the perception of the past event transforms into a healthier awareness and point of view.

This exercise can also apply to your romantic relationships. If your lover has cheated on you, however you ultimately decided to deal with it, you must let go of that negative chapter of your life. The chances are the person was just insecure and did not know what they wanted.

So many people try to fill an inner void in any way they can. So again, know that it is not personal.

I would like you to do this exercise with any unpleasant past event of your life that still keeps you in a destructive state of negativity. Try to relax and play a short movie, in your mind, reliving an unpleasant event from your past, even if it is very difficult to do so in the beginning. If you need a friend to be with you, have them with you so you feel safe.

During your movie, change the script and envision the person responsible for your past negative experience talking to you, in an open and honest manner. Have their dialogue resemble the truth, as you know it, about who they really are; a lost, desperate human being with very little awareness of their actions and its repercussions on others. Play out the movie, in your mind, until you begin to truly feel compassion, or some sort of positive feelings crop up.

Remember, it has to be real!

Also, keep in mind it does not matter how serious it was: abuse, rape, betrayal, infidelity; just remember it is never personal. This was a person who was permeated by all the negativity and evil that is rampant on our planet. If not you, it would have been someone else.

Please understand, I am not blasé or uncaring; I am totally aware of the gravity of such matters. If you have been raped or abused, the emotional trauma must have been devastating and it will have had a profound effect on your life. This is completely understandable.

But, and read this carefully — you must have a greater desire to be free, free from vindictive thoughts and free from resentment and hate. If you are not able to let go and forgive, you will not be able to move forward and, paradoxically, you will be forever connected to the lower vibrations (anger, revenge, violence, etc.) of the person who has harmed you.

On a practical level, these people cannot be excused and should face whatever punishment is just and deserved. However, for your own sake do not hate them, no matter what they have done to you. Instead, allow yourself to have compassion, because of your greater understanding of the present human condition and evolution.

Understandably, at first you will find it difficult to take all the negative perceptions and feelings of your past and convert them into positive ones. but you really need to understand the reasons why you are having this difficulty.

If you have not done what I have suggested in Chapter 2 and 3, when discussing the physical body, it will be more difficult to move forward because you are not 'in tune'. The less 'in tune' you are, the more difficult it is to grow in your spirituality.

The opposite is also true; if you are good about taking care of the health of your body through food and exercise, no matter what has happened to you in the past, you will be able to make a connection to something above the lower emotions of revenge, bitterness, hate, and so on. When this happens, you are moving away from a primitive condition and beginning to live in a state of conscious awareness.

CREATING AN INTERNAL CLEANSE

Another effective way to let go of past negative events and emotions is through the following breathing exercise:

1   Give yourself a few moments to relax.

2   Begin to inhale and exhale taking long, slow, deep breaths.

     As you exhale, imagine letting go of all the negativity from your past.

     Whatever it is you no longer want in your life (anger, revenge, jealously, etc.) let it all go completely.

     As you inhale, you want to breathe in all the positive qualities you need in your life now and in the future. Breathe in new qualities like calmness, courage and willpower; whatever you really need.

3 Continue this for a few minutes.

Occasionally when you breathe out, allow yourself to stay empty, without breathing in, for as long as you can. Now you are really able to feel the sensation of being free from past negative experiences. As you empty yourself, create an inner space and be inspired by what is about to follow when you refill that space with something new.

Occasionally as you breathe in, you will want to hold your in-breath for as long as possible and feel your lungs and body be filled with those new qualities of beauty, positivity and love — the inner qualities that you desire in your consciousness — really feel them, then exhale and continue.

Dealing with Forgotten Negative Experiences

You can do the previously mentioned exercises for all the past negative experiences that you can remember, but what about those negative experiences so traumatic they have been re-pressed and forgotten?

You can try to bring them to surface by therapy, hypnosis or some other customary method, but I suggest something very simple yet extremely effective; especially if you aspire to be in tune with the path of evolution.

For a few moments, repeat, in your mind or out loud when no one is around, a simple phrase (or 'mantra' if you prefer). It should go something like this:

I (your name) truly and freely forgive and let go of any negative event and person from my past; and anyone that needs to forgive me, now forgives me. I truly and freely forgive everyone and everything.

Repeat this as often as you can and connect with your Higher Self. I will explain more precisely what I mean by 'Higher Self' a bit later, but I am sure you have an idea of what I mean.

> *So be free, be happy and let it go. I really mean it. You are a beautiful human being in a process of evolution. Rise above this past primitive, darkness of the soul. Nothing can stop you. Help us all by becoming a being of light.*

You will eventually be able to feel and send pure and unconditional love for everyone, even those who have hurt you in past negative events you had managed to forget. Feel how beautiful it is to be in this state, then share your knowledge with others so they may enjoy the same emotional freedom.

SHARING UNCONDITIONAL LOVE

This is one of the most important things we can do immediately.

Everyday find some time when you can sit quietly for a few minutes and send pure, unconditional love.

1 Send it to yourself,

2 Then to the people you care for,

3 Then to every being, including those who have upset you the most.

  Just visualize for a moment this love in your heart and send it directly into the hearts of the people you are thinking of. Picture them in your mind basking in the light of consciousness.

4 Finally, send unconditional love into space.

At first this will not be so easy, but stick with it because, as you continue sending unconditional love to yourself and others, you will be pleasantly surprised at how much easier it becomes with regular practice. Please, do it for yourself and for all of us.

There will be people reading this who have constantly created evil and negativity in the past. If you are the abuser, the rapist, the cheater and so on, do not be too hard on yourself. If you are genuinely and truly beginning to understand the repercussions of your past actions, then forgive yourself.

You were a confused person, unconsciously connecting with a lower negative vibration. You had little awareness, frequently repeating previous patterns by doing similar negative things that had been done to you. If you are truly becoming more aware, you now know what to do. Repeat the same mantra of forgiveness as was just explained, forgive yourself and do whatever you can to live in the light of awareness from this point forward.

Regularly doing the exercises outlined in this chapter is the most effective, and quickest, way I know to deal with our negative states.

Go ahead, start today!

- Change your negative perceptions of the past through the movie exercise.
- Use the breathing techniques to let go of past negative experiences.
- Repeat the forgiveness mantra.
- Send unconditional love to every being.

I suggest you do this immediately while taking care of your body. You will find they are very effective in helping you connect with your Higher Self.

I think for the moment this is more than enough. If you are already doing something else, that is helping you move into a state of conscious awareness, that's fine; but please, also incorporate what you have learned in this chapter.

CHAPTER SEVEN

PERSONALITY

THE DIFFERENT ASPECTS OF OUR PERSONALITY

I have good news for you. You can be whatever you want.

Frequently the circumstances in our lives bring to the surface certain aspects of our personality. Over time we delude ourselves into believing this is actually who we are. It is not the truth. What we are experiencing is just a fraction of who we are and perhaps more importantly, who we can be.

Reflect upon the circumstances in your life that made you the person you are today; a different set of circumstances would have produced a different person. From this point forward, you should understand that our personality (who we believe we are) is the product of circumstances.

The funny thing is that, if you did have a different set of circumstances which would have resulted in a whole different personality, maybe you would have like it more...or maybe much less!

It really doesn't matter; it still would not be you anyway. What it is important to understand is that you are whatever aspect of your being you want to bring to the surface. Whatever you want to be, focus on it in your awareness and bring it to the forefront.

Easier said than done? Yes and no, but not as difficult as you might think, once you know how to do it. It all stems from the fact that our personality is made of many different factions often clashing; therefore inner conflict is the norm.

Once we realise different aspects of our personality can come to the surface and motivate our actions, we can start to take control. We need to be able to determine which aspect we want to enhance at any particular moment, and for how long.

Religions have talked about human beings having the freedom to choose between good and evil, but that is not the case. At present most of our thoughts and actions are quite unconscious. We actually have little awareness and spend most of our time in a state of semi-sleep. In this state we mechanically repeat old patterns and proceed through life guided by whichever aspect of our personality is in charge at any given moment.

Throughout life we develop certain habits and reactions to various circumstances which then become aspects of our personality which control our daily lives. We can see how this works in the following example:

One evening, the aspect of our personality that wants to lose weight may decide that the next day we will not eat anymore chocolate. At that moment we are in a calm state, thinking about our life and realizing this is best for our overall health. We feel determined and confident that we will be successful.

The next morning we wake up feeling lethargic. We are not looking forward to going to work, we drive through heavy traffic, and when we get there we are stressed. Then, we hear a little voice in our head that says *'Let's have a chocolate bar; I'm stressed, chocolate relaxes me, it makes me feel good'*

At this particular moment, the aspect of our personality that feels the need to have chocolate in order to feel good and relax, has surfaced mechanically. As usual, this has been triggered by previous events in our lives. It is a pattern that happens often, and unconsciously, within most of us.

The aspect of our personality that made the decision not to eat chocolate, the evening before, is nowhere to be found. This is because the current circumstances are different and, consequently, bring to the surface a different personality aspect that is connected to our past; the one from our childhood that tells us chocolate comforts us when we are upset.

In such situations one aspect can control our lives until another takes its place and, clearly, our habits are connected with our emotional states.

WHO ARE YOU NOW AND WHO DO YOU WANT TO BE?

To fully understand our varying emotional states, we need to look no further than ourselves. Who we are today, and how we behave, is triggered by external circumstances; the more powerful the circumstances, the stronger its influence on this aspect of our personality. Also, the greater likelihood it will take control of our life for a longer period of time. Therefore, we need to learn how to have better awareness.

Awareness is achieved when we begin to notice what circumstances trigger an aspect of our personality, combined with the realisation that we have the ability to stop mechanical responses and instead choose how we want to react. To take control of our lives we need to remember we are complex beings with many different facets often conflicting with one another. As a result, we have to create an inner chief, a being within us that makes the final decisions, in order to keep us on the right path of human evolution. As we move forward, through the rest of this book, I will refer to this inner chief as the 'Chairman', and later, I will introduce the 'Higher Self'.

Consider the life you have lived to this point. Look deeply within yourself and decide who you are and who you want to be. Take your time, because this is the biggest decision you will ever make.

Sit somewhere in silence and really examine your needs.

What would give you true inner fulfilment?

If a magic genie were standing next to you prepared to grant you one wish (one, not three!) so that you are given the particular need you so desire, what would you ask for?

Do not make up your mind until you are 100% sure (okay 99% sure is also fine).

Now, the aspect of your personality that really wants to fulfil that particular wish will now be the Chairman; the one who makes all final decisions towards becoming a true spiritual being. Anything else that you want (or the wants of other personality aspects) has to have the Chairman's approval.

Staying with our chocolate analogy, let's say you have to lose weight for health reasons. You, the Chairman, will call a 'meeting' and state from now on there will be no more chocolate. You will then sit in silence and listen, inwardly, to any aspect of your personality objecting. In fact, it is better to allow the aspect of yourself that likes chocolate to state its case: 'It tastes good', 'It relaxes me', 'It is a good substitute for the (perceived) love in my life', etc.

It is vital that you, the Chairman, explain that while those are valid points, you have made a decision for the overall good of your body and mind, and to continue this habit would result in future negative consequences. It is important that this decision be understood by every aspect of your personality if they are all to work together to achieve your goal.

The next time you have a stressful morning where circumstances trigger the aspect that wants chocolate, if we are fully aware of what is happening, we will connect with the Chairman to make sure we stick to our plan. If we are caught off guard, before we realise it we are already chewing...well, never mind, awareness is not achieved in one day alone! However, that evening the Chairman will again call a meeting to reiterate our intention to all the aspects and ask for their support.

The next time a similar situation arises, hopefully, the Chairman will intervene before the chocolate bar is unwrapped and make the final decision not to eat the chocolate. Great, if there is no resistance; but should there be, the Chairman will need to explain, again, the reasons why the decision has been made.

Each time, you will begin to notice, the aspect that wants the chocolate will protest less and less. Remember, these aspects are like small children looking for immediate gratification, with little understanding of future consequences. Patiently re-explain, to the aspect, the concept behind your decision.

Should the conflicting aspect of your personality stubbornly refuse the reasoning of the Chairman, you must be tough and uncompromising. Command respect and take charge, just as you would with a child; there is no flexibility for negotiation.

FINDING YOUR INNER CENTRE

As you strive to achieve your goals, you will encounter many aspects of your personality that can obstruct your progress. They have been created by past experiences, some negative and some positive.

Therefore, it is not usually a good idea to create a sole belief system or follow a particular aspect of your personality which you feel best fits with who you are and what you want to achieve. In order to carry on you have to manage all of them. You need to ensure they are in complete agreement and obedient to the Chairman. It will take a little while for the Chairman to become truly powerful and unmovable, but every time an aspect complies it will become easier.

The Chairman has to become the one and only voice in your life that matters if you are to become a true spiritual being and follow the path of evolution. When that happens you will feel an incredible inner strength, an immovable inner centre that gives you all the emotional love and security you need.

Throughout your life you have naturally desired to experiment, and this is fine. As long as there is no harm to others you should be free to explore. It is important to understand that when you create an inner centre, it makes it so much easier to experiment safely. Now, you have a home, somewhere to go back to, and much more confidence and inner security.

If you are truly serious about finding an inner centre, inner peace and a balanced way of life between internal and external success, you must ensure the Chairman aspect of yourself is able to fulfil these goals.

The Chairman has to be that part of you that has maturity, deep understanding and a nobility of intents; it is the sage inside of you. In certain ancient philosophies it is called the Higher Self because it is motivated by higher principles that concern the good of all. Any other aspect that is preoccupied with individual and egocentric benefits is considered as part of the lower self.

There is nothing wrong with the lower self, we need both the higher and lower selves in our lives, but just make sure the Higher Self is in charge. The other way round leads to trouble and that is exactly what is happening now; a bunch of self-centred children with barely an understanding of the wide-scale consequences of our thoughts and actions.

To reverse this process, we must start small. Once it is established that the Higher Self (the Chairman) is the only voice within us that matters, we can begin to understand the meaning of 'oneness', and all our thoughts and actions will automatically be for the benefits of all.

Of course you can do whatever you want and appoint an egocentric aspect of your personality as the Chairman, but I hope you do not. Even if, at first, that brings you some form of external success and satisfaction, it will ultimately take you away from the path and become a diversion from which you may take a long time to recover, if you do at all. This of course would create even more darkness for yourself and the whole world.

To achieve our urgent goal of placing the Higher Self in charge of our lives, we must become aware of which of our aspects are being triggered externally. Everything around us is a trigger and feeder for our complicated personalities.

Food provides a good example. It is important to realise that if our internal organs are not working properly our emotions will be affected, and will create a state of inner imbalance generating a particular aspect of our personality.

So, which type of food nourishes what? I would argue an unhealthy liver creates anger and thus the angry aspect of our personality. It is attracted by certain types of food that nourish it, like fried food or alcohol. Of course, the feeling of anger can also give us an energy to deal with certain threatening circumstances in our lives and, thus far, it may be perceived as a good thing, but only momentarily. In the long run anger will only create more inner imbalance.

In any case, this feeling is related to the aspects of the lower self and is definitely not conducive to any harmonious holistic outcome. The better way to find this energy is by letting the Higher Self provide you with the ideals and motivation to deal with life's challenges.

If you would like to know more about the correlation of internal organs and emotions, there are plenty of books available and resources on the internet. Even better, connect inwardly, listen and learn by personal experience. It is your responsibility to self-investigate and learn.

By the way, do not worry if it is not scientifically proven, experiment, be aware and soon you will find out what is fact or fiction, by yourself. When that happens, you will learn to place very little importance on the opinions of so-called scientific experts. Especially since most of them have no real, direct experience and sadly they are often not even interested in finding out. Become your own expert!

LISTENING TO YOUR HIGHER SELF

You are also your own doctor; and your body, mind, and consciousness are your expertise and laboratory of discovery.

Begin to find out which types of food feed your Higher Self best.

Once you learn this, the choice is yours, but at least you will now have a choice and be able to take responsibility for your actions.

Let's continue on with the process of self-awareness. Music is a good example because there are so many different types and they create such strong emotional responses.

Which type of music affects your being?
Why do you listen to one type of music over another?
What kind of sensation does it create within you?
What aspect of your personality is nourished by it?

Begin to notice patterns of what types of music you tend to listen to and their connection with your inner states. You will be amazed by your discovery. Just like eating certain foods, listening to certain music keeps us in a specific state of mind, related to the way we move through life.

When some people follow a musical genre it can also affect the way they look, dress and behave, but what we are discussing here is much more introspective than that. You will soon find out how the types of music and food that appeal to you are connected and feed the same aspects of yourself.

Similarly, begin to notice the kind of paintings, sculptures, poetry and so on that attract you and what they correlate with, inwardly. You may find you have different tastes in food, music and the arts, but all these different tastes vary according to your moods. What are moods if not just different aspects of us that come to the surface at certain times, triggered by certain events?

Here, however, is an important question to ask yourself:

Are these moods, aspects, choices of foods, music, arts connected with your Higher Self?

Are they nourishing your Higher Self, the one who will take you where you have decided you want to go?

Or, are they taking you in the wrong direction, often for the rest of your life?

Once you become aware of these answers, again the choice is yours to make.

If you are suffering from a serious addiction, realise it is not you who is addicted, but just one aspect of your personality.

This aspect, at the moment, is very powerful and behaves as if it is in charge, but that only happens because you have no inner Chairman who has the final word. In this situation, the aspect of your personality in question is out of control, and is behaving like a child with no guidance.

If you have not done so already, I encourage you to start, right now, and create the inner Chairman, however initially powerless, and persevere. Remember any doubts that enter your mind are not coming from you, they are created by the aspect connected with your addiction. Do not listen, they are lies. Only trust and listen to the voice of the Higher Self ...however faint.

Understand that you are not your aspect, you are so much more. Your aspect took control because of some past events or perceptions, but it has no real understanding, no knowledge; it is a lost, confused, misguided, tiny part of who you are as a being. Become aware and discover the real you; the one who you want to be. Take comfort in knowing that inside you are all the qualities and resources you need to be, on the path of spirituality; we all have this. Do it to take control of your own life, and help others to do the same.

It is also important to realise that not all these different moods and aspects are negative just because they are not directly connected with the Higher Self. You can continue doing many of the things you enjoy as long as the Higher Self is in charge and aware of what is happening.

It is a bit like how you might handle your children: *'Do your homework and then you can go play'*. The Chairman is always present, aware and responsible for the situation, not allowing things to get too far out of hand.

For a while, you should listen to your Higher Self, yet feel free to do the things you enjoy right now. It is important you do not completely deny yourself of the things that give you pleasure. Never do that, even if you realise they are selfish acts, but, at the same time, be very aware of the consequences.

Build on your connection with your Higher Self. Make sure it gets fed more and more, until the things that you find important, and which give you pleasure also give pleasure to your Higher Self. At the same time, the other, insignificant, things that now give you pleasure should become progressively less important and enjoyable. Soon you will see them for what they really are — child's play. We need to grow up fast if we want to get out of this mess.

I need to reiterate that the change has to be smooth and with awareness, do not force anything. Create and listen to the Chairman, within you, trust the judgement on when to work and when to play. Soon, everything you do will feel like playing, but it will be the Higher Self playing and that benefits everyone.

EMBRACING ALL ASPECTS OF YOUR PERSONALITY

We also have to realise the fragmented aspects of our personality are not enemies. They are just parts of who we are, at that particular moment, created by past experiences and repeating the same pattern because they know no better.

For example, the aspect of your personality that desires a cigarette has no intention of giving you cancer. It wants a cigarette because it helps you relax and often 'switch off' momentarily, from your daily routine. This aspect does not know any better. It is just like a small child. It is up to you, the Chairman, to explain and educate.

If you are stuck in traffic, in a taxi going to the airport, do not allow the aspect that worries and panics — if you still have not dealt with this aspect yet — to be in charge. There is nothing you can do but sit and wait for the traffic to move on.

Instead, allow the aspect that likes to sit still, listen to music or just breathe and relax to come to the surface. Do this and your experience will be much more pleasant. But you can only do it if you have an inner Chairman making the decisions.

Different aspects can also be quite useful in certain situations when you are in charge. One scenario might be if you are in a dangerous situation, you want to connect with the courageous and sometimes crazy aspect of your personality that can help you at that moment.

Look within yourself; you can access the various facets of the human experience and use them whenever you need to. If, at first, you do not find it within yourself, try to use a role model. For instance, if you cannot find courage inwardly, think of someone courageous you saw in a movie, or even in real life. You are looking for someone who gave you the 'wow' factor. Make a connection with the characteristics of this person and use it in your present situation.

Similarly, pay attention to the kind of man or woman to whom you are attracted.

What kind of characteristics do they possess?

Is there a pattern?

What does this tell you about yourself?

What does it tell you about your current decision making and the necessary adjustments?

Be honest and you will soon find out.

If you are a woman and you are looking for a man in your life to rescue you, what does it tell you about yourself?

The same question arises if you are a man and desire the woman who wants to be rescued; what does this tell you? (So you can feel 'manly?'?) Think about it.

In both cases we are dealing with imbalances, an aspect of your personality that has been created by a feeling of insecurity.

This aspect is in charge of your life and makes the major decisions; not a healthy place to be. Nevertheless, these two people will look for each other and create a co-dependent bond where each person does not face their real problems but, instead, creates an illusionary escape route. Ultimately, this behaviour will produce disharmony and the relationship will not last, or it will continue haphazardly because of their fear of being alone.

CHAPTER EIGHT

LOVE, SEX AND THE FAMILY

This is a time for another warning. If you find this chapter a bit preachy or 'instructional', please forgive me that was not my intention.

Nowadays, we confuse freedom with the notion of doing whatever we want to do. Of course, you can do whatever you want, but the only way to achieve true freedom is when we are an entire entity, when the Chairman is completely in charge and we are not at the mercy of various aspects of our personality. In this chapter I am touching on a suggested way of intimacy which will feed your Higher Self and help you along the path. Furthermore, I believe this mode of interaction will create the beginning of deep change in the way we all live, resulting in many positive repercussions.

As you work on developing healthy love in your life, remember there is no such thing as perfect love; you can only give as much love as you can master, in your present condition. Still, there are a few points I would like to share with you.

When we think about romantic love or 'falling in love' it usually involves having someone to satisfy our needs, to fill the voids in our lives and make us feel a bit more complete and in balance. That is what so many romantic movies and songs are all about; feeling complete with another person. However, when we are not in tune it is almost impossible to love unconditionally.

In order to really love we have to be more in balance, ourselves.

A lot of people do not love themselves but they love other people and this is pretty much impossible. When you do not love yourself there is incompleteness and a void that you believe will be filled by the other person (although it is never truly filled). This is why we get so possessive because, without the other person we have to go back to feelings of incompleteness, loneliness and the desperation of the human condition.

In order to experience romantic love, in the healthiest Way, we need to first have a clean body and mind and to be actively working on ourselves for a period of time, then we shall love the other person in a more balanced way. Love is not about filling our inner voids; it is about finding some other expression of life.

If you are a man, the female energy becomes very attractive so you want to nourish and support that energy. Basically it will be about giving. Contrary to how so many of us approach life, we do not need to receive in order to give and we do not need to be loved in order to give love. Once we give and express love it comes back to us naturally.

When we are in a healthy romantic state, loving is just an expression of sharing an inner state with another person who is pretty much on the same wave length. When we relate in that way love becomes very powerful in creating change, not only within ourselves but in the world.

OUR RELATIONSHIP WITH SEX

Another way to comprehend what a young species we are is by the way that we relate to sex. Our life is completely dominated by sex, to the point that many are not able to control their sexual urges. In order to obtain their goal, which is usually a quick, meaningless release, they often resort to dishonest behaviour leading to unhappiness. I compare it to a small child wetting the bed because they are not able to control that particular impulse. This is at the same level. We still seem unable to relegate this urge to its right place and time.

The act of sex is something that should be experienced and shared with another person as a component of a loving experience. we can see that the inability to control this impulse is absolutely connected with our consumption of certain foods, drinks, mind patterns and so on. Once again, achieving awareness is the key.

There is nothing wrong with wanting to satisfy different aspects of your personality as long as you, the Chairman, are in charge. You can have sex on impulse or whichever way you like. I am not big on making moral judgments so if you feel like ripping each other's clothes off and making love on the kitchen table covered in whipped cream...hey, whatever rocks your socks, great, do it and have fun. But, you must also know how to make love in a way that feeds your Higher Self.

You can do both and, eventually, you will lean more towards one way than the other. You don't have to force it, but whatever you do has to be real and what you really want. I am pointing this out because if you want to follow the path to consciousness it is important that awareness is present in the act.

Whatever physical expression your sexual experience assumes is not important. When we make love to another person it is such an intimate and beautiful experience. It is an amazing opportunity that allows us to get closer to each other and further our inner connection as well as our connection to others. This is a fundamental factor in the evolutionary journey.

I guess it should be clear by now that everything we do is for this purpose. It is what we are here to do. Honestly, what else is there to do? This is the path I believe we have to take. Yet, at the same time you are free to do whatever you like as long as you allow others the freedom to do the same.

Frequently, during the act of sex we tend to repeat patterns, including sometimes fantasizing about others. Too often we do not really meet during the act as we are preoccupied by other things in our mind or worried about our performance.

What does it mean to remain aware during sex? We simply continue the process of developing inner awareness by sharing it with your partner. If this sounds appealing to you, you may strive to have sex in the following manner:

Before the two of you engage in the act of sex take a few minutes to relax. Deep breathing will help and it will be even better if you look into each other's eyes. Gradually relax and begin to tune in to one another. Slowly begin exploring each other's bodies always maintaining awareness as you have learned and be receptive to your body's signals. Now become aware of the signals of your partner, as your goal should be to give maximum physical pleasure to your partner, while at the same time staying mentally connected to each other.

When the two of you are able to bond in this way, the crescendo leading to orgasm will happen as a natural consequence of this deep, intimate connection. Be totally focused on your partner and give unconditionally. If your partner does the same to you, you are both incredibly lucky to have found the other. It will not only be an amazingly beautiful experience, but you will also help each other in the process towards awareness.

BRINGING CHILDREN INTO THE WORLD

As a woman, be absolutely sure that you really want children; not every woman has to or wants to be a mother. The decision to have a child is yours and yours only, it does not matter what other people may think, or want, in your environment; and that includes your parents or partner/husband. Have children only if you desire to be a mother.

With this in mind, procreation is something for which we should prepare

Bringing children into our world can also be done with awareness, so we should prepare for the moment of conception at least three months in advance. We are realizing more and more that the key to our evolution is achieving consciousness.

Having healthy children that can achieve awareness is vital and we must do whatever we can to facilitate this process, and it begins as early as conception.

Hopefully, the two of you have already begun your path to consciousness and have applied all the things we have talked about so far. Three months before conception both of you should take extra efforts to make sure your bodies are as healthy as possible. Take care of your diet, maintain regular exercise and eliminate alcohol and cigarettes (I personally would avoid refined sugar as well).

As I have explained when talking about sex, you can do whatever you like. I am only suggesting a way to behave on the day of conception for those who may be open to some ideas.

As the day of conception approaches make sure you are in a peaceful state of mind. When the day arrives, do not eat too much; make sure your mind is clear. Create a warm and comfortable environment whatever that means for you, soft lighting, music, candles. You already know how to make love with awareness, so just take this state to the next level.

Sit facing each other and take full breaths and relax. Linger in this peaceful state for few moments. Stay in awareness of the fact you are getting ready to create a new life. Allow the love you feel for one another to fill the room. Sense it to the fullest and live these moments in total awareness. Then, slowly become one in your love making. There is nothing more to say...just be.

If you are reading with a conditioned mind you may perceive these suggestions as 'New Age' or crazy 'hippy' stuff. In reality it is an important, yet beautiful, way to express your awareness and freedom while being who you truly are.

Anyway, these are just my suggestions. As long as you take responsibility and apply conscious awareness to your actions, be free to let your intuition guide you in this magical moment.

THE PREGNANCY PERIOD

The pregnancy period is also very important. The mother should stay away from unpleasant images, movies, television programs and try to retain a state of tranquillity. Whatever is happening in your life, do not give it too much importance and just focus on being healthy, inside and out. Your child is your priority and for nine months it is your total focus.

If you are the father, you must take complete responsibility of the external circumstances. If there are problems, you must deal with them. Do not let anything worry your woman. Be a pillar of strength and give all your love, unconditionally. Ensure she can relax in the knowledge that you can be trusted completely. In this phase you are the protector. Take on this role with passion and nobility, being fully aware of what you are creating as a conscious couple.

The same applies for the first few years of the child's life. As the mother your energy and attention has to be focused on the child. During that time the mother's bond with the child is vital. A child needs to feel the strong, unconditional love of the mother in order to be nourished.

This takes a lot out of the mother, which is why it is so important that the father be an aware adult, not a man-child who starts to feel insecure when the mother's energy is suddenly more directed towards the child.

On the contrary, the man has to be able to fill the woman with love and affection, at all times, and in so doing replenish the love and energy that the mother is giving to the child. The father's love towards the child at this stage is also important, but it becomes even more relevant in later stages. This is why it is so important that a woman choose her partner carefully.

If you already have children, do not feel you have done something wrong if they were not conceived and gestated in this way. I do not want you to think, for a moment, that you have failed in any way, or that your children are any less for it. We can only do our best in any given situation, and never that of which we are unaware. You have an incredible amount of love and light inside of you, so give it to yourself and to your children. Do not worry; just take responsibility for the present. Help your children in their path to awareness, as they have all the resources they need inside of them; the past is irrelevant.

RAISING HEALTHY AND AWARE CHILDREN

You should raise your children with all the understanding and awareness you have acquired in your own path to consciousness — you know what to do. Children are, indeed, the future; we all know that, but what kind of future will depend on our approach to education.

We discussed the importance of having an inner centre in the previous chapter. It is important for children to also have an inner centre, early in life, for similar reasons — it will make it easier for them to go through life feeling more secure and aware.

As early as possible, you will want to explain the importance of food and exercise, to instil in them this understanding so they may avoid many physical and emotional problems later in life.

Awareness should be taught to your children, as early as possible: how to listen to their bodies, how to communicate with them, how to breathe and relax, and how to connect with the environment. Of course there is only so much you can do about external influences, but do the very best you can; it is all you can do at the moment. Hopefully things will change soon as more people become aware.

I have included a wonderful focus exercise in Chapter 12 that can also help children develop better awareness of the environment, rather than growing up feeling disconnected from it. If you are really serious about all of this, begin thinking about what you need to do for your children. If you have been through the process yourself, and understand what your body and mind needs in order to tune in, it will be so much easier to help your children achieve similar results. Similar results, though never the same, because your children will bring something new into the human experience. You know all the hazards, in this world, you want them to avoid; just use your common sense and under-standing — what worked for you, will work for them too.

Let your children grow with the least amount interference possible. Encourage them to develop creative and independent thinking rather than filling their minds with religious dogmas or scientific data.

It is fine if you have religious beliefs and you want to com-municate them with your children, but do not make them feel they must follow your ways without questioning their validity or keeping an open mind to different possibilities of belief.

The same applies to scientific thoughts. We cannot brain-wash our children to believe that science is the only valid way to understand ourselves and the environment, and that anyone who does not follow the, often rigid, scientific models is either ignorant or weird. If we do this we are just creating clones of ourselves. Instead, we should allow our children to have open minds and bring their own uniqueness into the world. Other-wise, there is no forward movement.

As a species, we have done a lot of crazy things throughout time and the results are clearly in front of us for all to see, nevertheless change can happen very quickly when we raise healthy and aware children. That is why the first few years of their life are so important; they provide the child with an inner core they will be able to connect to later on in life.

CHAPTER NINE

GAINING FOCUS AND AWARENESS

GOOD THOUGHTS, GOOD WORDS, GOOD DEEDS

In order to better understand what follows we have to become familiar with an ancient concept: at a certain point (and that point is now), evolution can only move forward if (right now) we follow a simple template:

GOOD THOUGHTS, GOOD WORDS, GOOD DEEDS.

Anything not in compliance with this principle will create evil.

Now, because we are in an early stage of our evolutionary journey as a species, it is very difficult to live in accordance to this template, therefore we produce evil constantly. That is why, in our present stage, evil is an unavoidable consequence. What does 'Good Thoughts, Good Words, Good Deeds' mean? These simple words mean what you read, there is no hidden connotation. However, when we begin to think about what it takes to put this idea into practice, it presents some challenges.

Even when we do our best to speak in a positive manner, or do good deeds in our day to day actions, they will never be completely natural, until we have positive thoughts *first*. Only when we are truly living in a positive state will our words and actions come from the right place.

In order to have positive, uplifting, thoughts we must have a certain degree of awareness and ability to focus. Even if I urge people to start doing this immediately, having and retaining positive thoughts is quite difficult, and verges on impossible if we have not yet focused on the previous stages discussed so far.

That is why we really have to do our best to create a balanced body and mind condition, otherwise our negative thoughts and emotions will get in the way of forward progress. Our best intentions will be wasted, and as a result we will become defeated and disillusioned with our inability to be, and remain, in a positive, loving inner space.

We have already decided that we must create our inner Chairman. During the day we have to do our best to have positive thoughts, words and deeds, but it will take a while before we are doing it most of the time. If we connect more and more with the Chairman, during our day, it will be easier to remain focused and ensure our actions are motivated by the Higher Self.

Often it is not easy because our interactions with others are not always smooth. Frequently, we can find ourselves being dragged into conflict situations and our automatic reactions take over. Then we find ourselves saying or doing things we know we should not.

It happens automatically because these behavioural aspects have emerged many times before in similar situations, creating and renewing old negative energies. In doing so, this pattern goes on to feed the darkness that we are now experiencing on the planet.

During the evenings, it is very important to look back at all your daily activities and interactions. This is important, so begin doing this as soon as you can. First connect with the Chairman and relive in your mind the disharmonious events of the day.

You want to become aware of the instances where you were caught in a spiral of negativity. Whatever happened, change the script; then relive the event the way you would have wanted it to unfold, if the Chairman had been in charge at all times. Take your time; make sure whatever negative feelings you created and experienced are transformed into something positive and harmonious. Do this for as long as it takes.

Before you go to bed you have to be free from any negativity from the day. You have to be sure that at the end of the day you have created and sent into the planetary field more light than darkness. It is essential that the ratio be changed towards positivity, particularly before you go to sleep. When you go to bed, you have to be in a positive space. You do not want it to contain any residue of negativity. You must make sure any negative thoughts have been transformed into positivity so that, during the sleeping hours, you are in a harmonious state.

If you do take negativity to bed, your sleeping pattern will be affected. Your dreams will not be harmonious and you will awake with similar negative thoughts to begin the new day. You must make certain that positivity fills you so that you can to ensure you sleep like a baby.

THE FALLACY OF POSITIVE THINKING

We must not confuse positive behaviour with the 'turning the other cheek' concept. The truth is we have to be like warriors. One of our primary purposes is to be positive and to try to help others help themselves. Nevertheless, sometimes we may be caught in a situation when the right thing to do requires excessive behaviour. We have to stand our ground, in any situation, and not be taken for granted, or bullied, because of our desire to create positivity.

When needed we have to be firm and uncompromising; if that leads to a verbal or physical fight (hopefully not), you have to do whatever it takes to defend yourself, and maybe others, because it is the right thing to do. Do not confuse this with anger; anger is personal, justice is not.

Later on, you should send pure, unconditional love to the person in question. While I suggest you stay away from inharmonious people, it does not mean you do not love them, it just means you have to love them from a distance!

GAINING FOCUS AND AWARENESS

I also want to talk about another fallacy of positive thinking.

There are quite a few books discussing the power of the mind, positive thinking and so on. Personally, I have found most of them can be quite misleading. It is true that if you focus on something for a certain amount of time you can achieve it.

The problem is, how can we do that when our minds are operating in a mechanical state? When we have a lot of confusing, often conflicting thoughts swirling around in our minds, it is difficult, if not impossible, to focus on anything for more than a few seconds.

Even if you try, during the day, to spend some time on positive thinking, as soon as you begin to do something else, your mind goes back to the same old mechanical, repetitive patterns. These patterns are often depressing because of previous negative experiences; then add in the fact that our bodies are not healthy, which affects the quality of the blood that flows into our brain; moreover, if our muscular structure is not equally developed, further imbalances and tensions are created.

We have to be realistic and take responsibility. We cannot achieve anything, of real substance, if we are not prepared to follow the basic steps of healthy living. I have seen so many people who are verging on delusional, believing they can live and think in a positive space, while neglecting the basic care of their body and mind.

I apologize if this sounds overly simplistic but, if your liver is overworked, or your mind is still affected by past negative experiences, it will be extremely difficult for you to have meaningful, positive thoughts, which can create a difference in the environment.

So many people talk about love, especially in religious groups, but we have to remember that true love always creates positive behaviour and harmony. Many people profess that their belief systems are founded on love and God, and thus they have received Jesus, or other saviours, according to the convictions in their heart. If that is the case they should not have negative thoughts in their minds and words. Their actions should be motivated by their love for all.

If you still find yourself jealous, bitter or indulging in any emotions that are not based on unconditional love for all, regardless of religion, beliefs, race, social status and the like — do not fool yourself; there is no saviour in your heart. Take responsibility for your life and work towards tuning in to a more enlightened state.

On the other hand, if you are truly able to love unconditionally and create harmony then it does not matter what belief system you follow; you are doing fine. And if you are in this state, looking after your body and mind the way I explained, this should come as a natural consequence.

THE POWER OF CONCENTRATION

Here is a simple but very effective three minute exercise to develop your power of concentration, and as a result it will allow you to remain in an aware positive state for increasingly longer periods of time.

1   Take an A4 sized sheet of white paper.
2   Draw a circle as big as the sheet will allow with a black felt pen.
3   Completely fill the circle with the pen until it is completely darkened. Please note it is very important that the circle is black because it helps concentration, any other colour will only distract your attention and create fantasy images in your mind.

4   Sit on the floor or a chair with your back straight, and
     with the sheet placed in front of you at eye level.

5   Slowly breathe in and out prolonging each breath to
     seven seconds pausing for a second between the two
     phases.

6   While you are slowly inhaling and exhaling, make sure
     you are looking at the black circle at all times. Do not
     allow your eyes and mind to wander. If you realise this
     is happening, immediately return to the black circle
     and keep your focus permanently on it for the entire
     three minutes.

By maintaining your focus on the black spot you are training
yourself to remain awake, and in the present. We have to learn
to remain awake in the present for longer periods of time, in
order to increase our power of concentration, and as a result
make sure our positive thoughts are powerful and effective.

Do not focus on the black circle for more than three
minutes. Believe it or not, for some to remain focused for three
seconds is an achievement, so working up to three minutes will
take time and effort. What you can do, if you wish (and I
sincerely hope you do), is to repeat the exercise during the day;
three times a day would be ideal.

After you begin doing the exercise, start to notice during
your day if you are staying in the present more often. If you
notice your mind and emotions taking you somewhere else, for
a moment see in your mind the black circle, and try to stay in
the present, with the awareness of where you are and what you
are doing.

Of course, there are so many situations in life that may affect us and which contribute to the negativity in our actions,
words and thoughts. This is true, but it is also untrue. We have
to stop believing that life is so complicated. It is actually very

simple; if we are in tune. It is as if there is a beautiful tree outside our window, but we are all so short-sighted that all we can see is the tree's 'blur'.

Many 'experts' will formulate different hypothesis and conflicting opinions of what that blur is. These divisions, and far out ideas, only create more confusion; all we need to do is restore our own clear sight and then the tree will reveal itself in all of its simplicity.

The funny thing is so many best-selling books are, and will continue to be, written by short-sighted people who will feel important because their opinions are shared and consumed by a large group of people, but just like the authors of these books they are just confused and only searching for an answer to the blur.

Before you write a book or give a seminar you have to make sure you live what you preach. There are so many books written by people without any real knowledge, simply regurgitating what they have read before. It is dishonest behaviour that brings even more confusion, or at best, a limited vision and often an unrealistic understanding of the true spiritual path.

There are a lot of false teachers around. Some are unconsciously misleading, and in some ways they are more confused than dishonest; and others, the dishonest ones, are consciously aware of what they are doing being simply motivated by the usual old world attractions of money and power.

It is up to you to sort what is real from what is not and to do it in any situation. The best way to do this is through having a healthy body and mind, and clear sight will come as a result. It will then be easy for you to see through the mask of deception some people seem to wear.

We have to stop being fooled by charismatic individuals with little substance. There are many around, especially politicians. Words and promises are cheap. Pay attention to what a person does, not what they say. In order to see the tree clearly we have to tune in, just like a radio station playing at the right wavelength.

If we are using such a small amount of our full capabilities, how can we know if we have clear sight or know what is the right or wrong thing to do? It is true we are in an early stage of evolution but, whatever the reasons we are here, we seem to have the ability to understand our limitations and work within them by tuning into our human vibration (or wave length). By doing this, we create the optimal condition to allow evolution to take its course while, at the same time, become sufficiently equipped to face the new challenges which our 'growing up' will create.

In other words, let's do the right thing so we do not stray from the path. We have to be and remain in tune, so that we will always have within ourselves the necessary resources to clarify and face the challenges of our journey towards full human potential.

Essentially, the 'blur' is the tree in our analogy and 'clear sight' is the capacity to see it clearly for what it is in the present moment. As we evolve, the tree will become something else, but by then we will have the capabilities to see it for what it is at that stage.

CREATING A STATE OF AWARENESS

What it is also important to comprehend is that, up to now, human evolution has had happen in a mechanical, instinctual, animal-like manner; but that is as far as it goes. From now on, evolution can only unfold through conscious awareness.

There is nothing wrong with the way we are now, or have been in the past; even if our past was filled with wars, cruelty, oppression and injustice — it was unavoidable. It was due to our evolutionary process and our still primitive state of consciousness.

We have to look very carefully at the way we still hang on to outdated models of the past. We need to understand it is time to let go of these archaic perceptions of life and replace them with an awareness of our thoughts and actions.

No one is really 'bad', we are in evolution, so we still carry the animal instinct for survival combined with a tiny amount of awareness. So at this stage, our primary focus of individual survival often comes at the detriment of others. Additionally, the desire to have power and control over others is a primitive mechanism that does not account for true conscious awareness; we all are made of a single consciousness, perceived as separated, by our limited senses.

Our negative actions, and the negative thoughts we harbour in our minds, affect all of us. Those who partake in such thoughts and behaviours for an illusionary gain, or advantage, they seek to acquire are truly ignorant. Again, forgive those who are not able to truly understand the repercussions of their actions.

There is nothing wrong with religion. It has fulfilled an evolutionary need in the past, despite the division and suffering its followers created, because it has been balanced by the hope and reassurance they have brought to so many, in our early stage of evolution.

The fact is, there is no longer a need for religion, because the new phase of evolution can only be achieved through consciousness. It is now important for everyone to connect with their inner human nature. It is necessary to tune in to our universal wavelength and avoid any kind of external divisions and conflicts that are created by religious beliefs. There is no longer a need to belong to a religious group. To be a member of the human race involved in the process of evolution is what will give us now, and in the future, hope, inner security and fulfilment.

When we feel connected, and in tune, there is no further psychological need for external securities and the religious belief of a God. There is no need to believe in Gods because, if we are in tune with human nature and the path of evolution, a God will not be an external thing; rather an inner acknowledgment and understanding that does not need to be verified by external religious beliefs of any kind.

Modern technology is another factor that inhibits our self-awareness and is magnified in our limited level of evolution. Mobile phones, computers, televisions, and the like are slowly taking us further and further away from an inner connection. We are becoming more out of tune.

Because we are still like children our capacity for focusing and concentrating is very limited so we easily get sucked in and lose ourselves when watching television or 'surfing the net'. Therefore, we should always keep the focus on ourselves; be aware of ourselves and what happens around us especially when dealing with such apparatus.

When you are watching television, or using computers, try to remain in a state of awareness. You can do this by keeping your attention divided between what you are doing and the rhythm of your breath. It means you do not lose the awareness of where you are and what is happening around you; you do not become a 'zombie' completely drawn into the screen.

You have to remain awake and keep the inner connection at all times. It is a form of self-acknowledgment that you exist at all times. Do not fall into a state of awakened sleep. By being fully awake in, the present, we are in complete control of our lives. If we lose ourselves, we are not centred anymore, and open to any kind of conditioning and brainwashing that may come through the screen.

Let us not be hard on ourselves; small children create a mess in their rooms and we have done the same with ourselves and our environment. But the mess must be cleaned up. It needs someone not only to point it out, but we also need men and women with an understanding of the solution. They have to be willing to do it, despite so many still wallowing in the mess with no understanding or desire to change it, and sometimes ridiculing those who are.

But it does not matter. When you are in tune you also understand you have no choice but to be truthful to yourself regardless of consequences. If you are not able to do so, do not despair, it simply means you are not completely connected yet; persevere and you will be. In the meantime, please do the best you can. We really need to create a directional change right now. We need to grow up fast, avoiding responsibility, like little children, is no longer acceptable.

Can you imagine what would happen if a group of small children are left alone in a house; it would get messier by the minute. Very soon not only would there be chaos, but after a while the children themselves would feel uncomfortable and temperamental. They would begin to miss the adults who could restore order and security in the environment.

We are much the same. As a young race we are very chaotic and unaware of the consequences of our actions; but unfortunately we have the capability to create mayhem and destruction on a much larger scale. The greater danger comes from our belief that we are adults aware of our actions. We are actually quite arrogant in our assumed greatness, as the most advanced form of life, when we have done nothing to achieve it.

First of all, we are far from advanced, because we are in a very early stage of evolution; perhaps one day we will be, but we are certainly not right now. In fact, most of us are oblivious to the hard work that is necessary in order to fulfil our potential as a species. Right now we are using a fraction of our potential and the danger is obvious. To deviate from the path of evolution, as we are doing right now, and to continue in this perilous direction can only lead us to a dead end.

Because there are no 'adults', we have to clear up this mess ourselves; just like a small child who can only clean up its mess if it has achieved a glimpse of discipline and understanding, we can only do it if we have achieved a fraction of the awareness that will move us forward.

The mess we have created in our bodies and environment is not only physical, but above all — energetic. The vibrational negativity and darkness that surround us has to be addressed, immediately, before it becomes irreversible.

I remember an advertisement for a hand-held computer game saying something like, 'Wherever you are...be somewhere else'. Why do we have this desire to escape all the time? We seem to be drawn towards whatever takes away from our present state and this is because we are not satisfied, and how could we be?

Alcohol, drugs or whatever can give us a respite from our condition, regardless of our social or financial status, it makes no difference. Do not believe for a second if you were rich or famous it would be any different; it wouldn't. The rich and famous have far more means and ways to escape reality and that is actually a disadvantage.

For them, no matter many personal or emotional problems they may have, the distractions of wealth, fame and the adoration of so many, usually makes the task of dealing with their problems less urgent and a bit more bearable in their day to day life. Consequently, it takes an extraordinary person to resist escaping their problems and following the spiritual path, when there are so many available opportunities to feed their ego. There are those who are exceptions to this but, on the whole, be grateful that you have very few means to escape, rather than envying those who have many. If you have an artistic gift, its fulfilment may lead you to fame and fortune, which is fine, because it is a natural consequence of expressing who you are.

But to chase fame and fortune, just for sake of enjoying fame and fortune, is a shallow endeavour that will only take you away from your true self. If you wish to achieve an inner connection do not chase illusionary dreams of grandeur or success because you are much better off as you are now; and that is much closer to the truth. As one famous artist said in one of his songs, 'When you have nothing, you have nothing to lose'.

Following an external illusion will be likely to take you away from true fulfilment, instead, start the process of inner connection. As you become more and more in tune you will find the need to escape will lessen and you just may discover the pleasure derived from being in tune will be stronger than any escape route could ever be.

Becoming Aware of Your Body Signals

This is an exercise to help you become more aware of your body internally and externally. When you are more in tune you can better take responsibility for its care:

1   Allow yourself to relax in a quiet and serene space and focus on your fingers. You might begin with the thumb of your right hand.

    Focus on it until you can really feel it. Feel it become different from the rest of your body. You will start to feel a sensation.

2   Then move on to the next finger, and so on.

3   Next shift your focus to your left hand, then your toes, neck, shoulders and so on. Isolate the body part and connect with your mind until you begin to feel a sensation. You may even notice how one body part may feel warmer or colder than the other, but it is all about developing awareness of your body.

4   Focusing on your internal body parts is a bit more
     difficult but you are still going to use your mind to
     focus on your internal organs. Really begin to feel your
     liver, your heart, your spleen and any internal body
     part you choose until you can identify its separateness

I have stressed earlier in this book the importance of recogniz-
ing the signals your body sends you when certain types of food
are not good for you, such as when you feel a twitch in your liver
from eating fried foods.

Once you are able to make a connection with your body
inside and out, it will be easier to recognize its signals and make
the necessary changes.

CHAPTER TEN

WHY WOMEN ARE THE FUTURE

Ok, time for another warning. I know that some will feel uncomfortable with this chapter and, because of conditioning, others may think that I am bias against men. Nothing could be further from the truth. So, in order to remove any misunderstanding I will explain in a simple manner what follows.

Male energy is more extrovert and female more introvert, that is why women are better at expressing their feeling then men by being more in touch with them. In the next stage of evolution men and women have to express, in an outward manner, female qualities like compassion, unselfishness and unconditional love in order to create a much needed change in the way we live.

By following the path of healthy body and mind as previously explained in this book we, men and women, will be able to tune in to our healthy male and female nature. Women will be able to connect with their healthy female qualities and man have to help them (instead of suppressing them) to be more extrovert in order to be able to express these qualities in every aspect of our lives and create a change in society. Men have to embrace the female energy within themselves and in women and of course women have to help them in this process.

A healthy man that embrace his female energy instead of suppress it will NOT loose his male energy, on the contrary it will be enhanced and become a better quality of male energy, strong and gentle and he will feel completed.

In the next stage of evolution female energy has to be the leading force in women and men. Of course women have a stronger female energy within them then men. That is why in the next stage of evolution women have to help men to embrace the female energy.

In order for this to happen we need healthy women that are willing to acknowledge their powerful female energy and be willing to express it freely and fearlessly. We also need healthy men that are in touch with their powerful male energy and are mature enough to understand that they need to embrace, cultivate the female energy in themselves and allow women to help them in this process.

By allowing healthy women to lead us in the next stage of evolution we will create a much better world where we will address the current unbalance and both male and female will live together in a state of balance and harmony.

My apologies If you feel that what follows it's a bit harsh. I feel I need to get your attention. There is no time to "beat around the bush", still now we are stuck in a damaging mindset where female energy has not been given it's proper relevance and we need to readdress this issue immediately. Change has to happen soon and I believe too many people are not taking this issue seriously enough when it is of paramount importance for our survival.

Remember there is no war of the sexes, men and women are not enemies; we have to become the best of friends, overcome our fears and forget our egos and be mature enough to understand and acknowledge what can be done to move forward harmoniously. If sometimes makes you feel uncomfortable try to understand why. We are talking about thousand of years of conditioning; to feel uncomfortable is to be expected.

THE IMPORTANCE OF FEMALE ENERGY

Male society and religions have brainwashed women to believe they need men when right now it is actually the opposite. Basically many men are emotionally afraid of women and of female energy because they cannot understand it.

The predominance of male energy on the planet was probably unavoidable...until now. The primordial path of evolution was based on fighting for survival, against the environment, different tribes, villages and later on, countries. This phenomenon was due to the primitive level of consciousness that we had to experience as a new species.

In this environment, the male energy (also present in women) of being more self-centred, less compassionate and more outwardly cruel was the necessary driving force that brought us to where we are now; even if in a, sometimes, horrific manner.

That time is over; male energy alone cannot take us any further. We are moving into a different phase of evolution, in which the predominant forces will be female energies like compassion, unselfishness and universal love. At present, the ugly side of male energy is still running the show, and that is why we are in danger. Women have to realise immediately they are the key to our future; female energy has to be the leading force.

Unfortunately, there is a strong imbalance between male and female energy. As we have seen with many women in the past, they have been conditioned to be dependent on men influenced by the draconian laws of male-oriented societies. This primitive state of affairs, combined with the need for a woman to feel secure and protected when raising a family, has created the present pattern.

It is time for a radical change, because the evolution of our species can only proceed when women realise their inner strength, and are free to achieve their full potential, without fear of upsetting the male ego and its norms.

The woman who takes the responsibility of connecting with her Higher Self becomes a very powerful being who needs no one to rescue her. She will want in her life a similar man — someone who has found his own inner centre and strength and desires someone to share his experiences.

The enlightened man will not want someone to control. He will not want a woman who overlooks his weaknesses and insecurities, so often disguised through financial and social status or macho behaviours. The insecure man, who wears this thinly disguised mask of superiority, will eventually be revealed as a scared, insecure child; unfortunately, just another child that a woman will have to deal with, in her family.

It is time for women to put an end to this ridiculous pattern, to stop accepting this 'boys will be boys' nonsense. Do not put up with the patronizing behaviour of many men any longer. Do not excuse it. It does not help them and it does not allow you to grow. There's not a weakest sex; that is complete nonsense.

Male and female energy have different, yet complementary, characteristics when expressed by women and men in a mutual state of inner harmony.

We must realise that, in order to further evolve, female energy has to become the driving force in the planet. This unique energy is about giving, sharing, and above all, unconditional love; things most women experience naturally. Even in an unbalanced state women seem to be able to tune into this energy, when it comes to their children; men cannot do this, right now they possess and express mainly unbalanced male energy. Therefore a man's love is almost always conditional no matter how much we want to sugar coat it.

THE NEW WOMAN AND MAN

Women and men possess both female and male energies. Women have mainly female energy with a bit of male in it, and the opposite is true for men. This is the general pattern, but some of us have more energies of the opposite sex than others. Unfortunately, we do not have many examples of healthy male energy; however, a man ruled by the Higher Self (the Chairman) will express a healthier quality of male energy.

He will be kind, noble, honest, reliable, courageous, responsible, ready to fight against injustice and prepared to sacrifice his life for those he loves. It's a bit like the knights, or heroes, in fairy tales or mythology. As a woman, why wouldn't you want a man like this? Well, we will come back to this point shortly.

Unhealthy, unbalanced male energy is the opposite — cruel, dishonest, controlling, violent, cowardly, irresponsible, and self-centred. Nowadays, we have too many examples on the planet of unbalanced male energy creating wars, injustice or craving insane control over others. Right now, male energy is sick and out of control and it is very dangerous for our future.

Female energy when healthy, is harmonious, elegant, gracious, giving, sharing, soothing, all embracing, and all loving; a bit like the noble princess in the fairy tales (but not the helpless one in the tower who always needs to be rescued). However, unbalanced female energy is not so different than the male, although more subtle and introverted. Her distorted energy will result in more scheming, passive controlling and manipulative behaviour.

Until now, unbalanced male energy has been the ruling force in the process of evolution. Being more extroverted was necessary, in our first phase; the suppression of the female energy was an unfortunate consequence but probably unavoidable, in this primordial phase. Now that we are out of the jungle and slowly achieving a state of consciousness, female energy has to be the leading force; it is our only way out.

The woman has to start the process of inner connection and connect with her Higher Self in order to discover her own true, powerful female energy. Once this is realised, she must nourish it and express it in her everyday actions. Conversely, from now on, women must demand that men do the same. Men tend to find it difficult to connect inwardly because of social and behavioural conditions and expectations. Help is at hand because, in this next stage of evolution, spiritually, the female energy has to lead and the male follow.

The next stage of evolution, led by the Higher Self, will be about oneness and unconditional love for all beings. Women need to help men through this process and men should accept it with pride, understanding and gratitude. A true man will embrace it rather than fear it.

As we approach the next stage of evolution, the doors to the female mystery will open. The only reason it has been perceived as a mystery, in the first place, is because the female energy has already been rooted in the next stage of evolution, and, as a species, were not there yet. Male energy is simple but, it is embedded in the past.

This learned attitude that the male is in some sort of position of superiority, simply has no merit in the next stage of evolution, and certain changes need to be made immediately. For instance, nowadays, when women and men get married the woman takes on the man's name, but why? This continues to feed into the philosophy of male importance. Furthermore, if you consider it in terms of biology, women are the ones who give life, gestate and feed the infant in the early stages and unlike men, we always know who the mother is; they are the ones who carry on the process of evolution in a way.

For these reasons, I strongly believe it should be the woman's name that is carried on. At the very least, it should be both names, but women should not give up their family names. If we seriously intend starting the process of female energy prominence in the next stage of evolution, this is an important step towards the resurgence of female energy.

Throughout the current media this assumption of male superiority continues to persist. Movies still have too many examples of helpless females who need to be rescued, even if that is slowly changing. It is important that women are seen as stronger, more independent and able to look after themselves, both practically and emotionally. So many little girls have been brainwashed by negative female 'role models' in the entertainment industry; it is time to reverse the trend so girls can grow up with a different mindset.

I encourage all women to look after their body and participate in some sort of fitness exercises. I have already explained which ones I believe to be the best, but you may also want to include some martial arts or self-defence courses in order to feel more self-assured and stronger within your body. This will have additional positive effects on your mind and psychologically you will feel stronger and more independent.

It is incredible how powerful the mind is and how it can shape our reality. Women are not what we see at the present time; they are powerful beings who have been conditioned to see themselves as weaker and often helpless, and if you insert that belief continuously in someone's mind it will become their reality. It is time to get rid of this lie and harmful negative programming.

I cannot emphasise enough how important is to understand the concept that from now on the female energy must lead and the male follow. Any man who understands this and is ready for the next stage, should do everything he can to help women achieve their potential. We need to help women to connect, live and express true, uplifting female energy so they can help us evolve further.

When you see other men behaving in outdated macho, controlling and insecure ways, do not feel that you have to play their game in order to fit in. Why would you even want to fit in with something so simple-minded and primordial? Instead, point it out and denounce it for what it is. Be brave and be truthful to who you are and what you feel. You are the man of the future. If you can, help them to also become men of the future, because a real man will not allow others to mistreat women. He will highlight the injustices that women are still subjected to, around the world. He will treat every woman with respect, kindness, honesty and devotion as they are potential princesses — this is a true expression of healthy male energy.

Let there be no misunderstandings. The new man I am describing is no wet blanket or an insecure, passive person who needs a woman to 'tell him what to do' or whom some people will call a 'wimp'. Quite the opposite; he is a warrior of peace, strong in body and mind, healthy, positive, caring, courageous, filled with an inner sense of justice and ready to do everything he can for the woman he loves and cherishes.

At the same time he has a mature awareness to accept the woman's help with pride and nobility. This does not mean a man should blindly treat a woman like a princess. Right now the female energy in women is far from healthy. Women have to, first and foremost, work on themselves to discover their inner centre and connect with their female energy so they understand what it is needed from them.

Women do not find it easy to connect with this energy because it has been repressed for such a long time. Women, need to make sure they are on the path of true spirituality, then they can help men to become real men of the future, continually supporting them and reminding them, when they lose their way, that we are all works in progress and we have to help each other.

THE ULTIMATE SEX TABOO

One of the most important social aspects we need to rectify quickly is the way men and women relate to sexuality. For thousands of years, women have been submissive to men and, for most of the world, not much has changed; this includes the western world where things are far from ideal.

However, there has been a growing proliferation of web-sites, adult clubs and holiday retreats based on the S&M lifestyle where many women are taking the dominant role and men the subservient one.

There is a belief that only a tiny minority of men are inter-ested in this role-reversal, but that is far from the truth. The unspoken and repressed desire to be dominated by a woman is quite widespread, and there are reasons why this is the case. Men have grown up with the false concept that they are stronger than women, just because they are physically stronger (this too is changing), and also by the way women have being oppressed through the ages. To this day it is widely accepted that a woman would like a man to 'sweep her off her feet', that the reverse is quite unthinkable...or is it?

Can you imagine a man talking to his friends and expressing this desire? He could never mention it or admit it. He would get strange looks from both men and women; yet, it is quite a common desire within men, which nobody talks about.

Unconsciously, men realise that women have a stronger emotional centre and that they need to understand and embrace the female energy and let it become the driving force in the next evolutionary phase. However, men are afraid to do it because of present environmental influences and the fear of losing their main source of self-esteem, the perception of being the stronger sex.

Unlike women, who can do it openly, men are not, current-ly, in the position to openly fulfil any desire of being swept away by a strong woman and the powerful female energy they sense in her. Instead they do it secretly by paying a professional dominatrix, or joining a similarly themed private club or website.

This unbalanced situation could be easily solved by men connecting with the healthy male energy within them and having relationships with women who are also in touch with their healthy female energy. If this were the case they would sweep each other off their feet whenever the desire was there. It would be two healthy beings, unafraid and unashamed, happily and completely surrendering to the noble knight and princess in each other.

When you feel this way about women, you will want to point out the injustices that women are still subjected to and do what you can to help them in every aspect of life. Do not focus only on your mistress because you find her sexually attractive, instead 'serve' all females; it is long overdue.

So my suggestion, to the man looking to be dominated is first, to become a healthy example of male energy, then you can 'serve' the woman of your dreams with nobility and devotion. Right now, female energy has to be the leading force, but the woman that embodies this energy has to lead with love, compassion and wisdom.

What can I say to the professional dominatrix? You can do whatever you want, and use the power that men give you for your personal benefit. You can enjoy being treated like a queen by passive followers, but your potential can be so much more magnificent.

You could work to become an example of healthy female energy. You could use your power to help men to understand it, appreciate it and embrace it. You can teach them how to become men who treat women with dignity, passion and respect. You could also let your followers know they can indeed serve you (if that is what they want), but in a proud, noble and dignified manner.

You are in a powerful position. Do not exploit men like they have women throughout time, and still do. You are much better than that. There are men who look up to you and listen to you; use your power to create a change that will benefit future men and women. As a woman you are potentially the one who can bring light to the planet; do this and your 'submissives' will follow.

CHAPTER ELEVEN

FOLLOWING THE PATH OF EVOLUTION

NEW AGE MANIA

The proliferation of New Age books has created an approach to spirituality that is not based on anything particularly authentic or truly attainable by the masses. It becomes a cult as people begin wearing a perceived 'New Age' style of clothing and communicating with their new found vocabulary. This is actually the opposite of what spirituality is all about. Spirituality is about freedom of expression and not being tied down to any set of ideas or images. Many people believe this is the way to become spiritual, and they could not be more wrong.

There are so many far-fetched ideas and vague concepts, based largely on wishful thinking: the idea that we can achieve anything if we want to; we are amazing beings of light, and everything is going to be all right because the universe is full of love; we are moving towards an age of enlightenment in which the earth will be a paradise, and we will all live together in peace and harmony.

Beautiful thoughts, aren't they? No wonder Scientists, and their like, think these kinds of views are loony; I can't blame them.

Unfortunately, it is not that easy. All these wonderful concepts are not based in reality, because the present level of awareness is almost nonexistent. The concepts are not farfetched in themselves, not at all. I do believe one day, when we achieve our full human potential, we will be able to do unimaginable things and, indeed, live in a state of loving harmony inconceivable in our present state.

We must keep our feet on the ground. Having intuition does not make you a psychic; a coincidence does not mean your life is guided by some inner knowledge which leads you to certain places, to do certain things and meet certain people — all because it is your destiny.

Too many people in the New Age movement are looking for a quick emotional pay off, without taking responsibility for their own lives. The reality is that most of us do not even know where our liver is, never mind being aware of its needs.

We have problems sleeping, we eat too much, we cannot control our cravings, we are not aware of our thoughts and the repercussions of our actions; we usually go through life mechanically being led by instinct or habits. We have little awareness of ourselves, and certainly not much of an inner connection; many of us are a mess. People who are not aware, or do not want to accept our present condition, love New Age ideas, because they float aimlessly in the air and do not require any real inner work.

It is much the same for those who blindly follow rigid scientific dogmas or the other various religions, organized or not. I think it is great to have so many people believe in New Age concepts, I love this enthusiasm, but I suggest you try to understand what you need to do now. Start from the beginning and work within your limits. Even if you experience a small improvement, which is much better than a fantasy with no real foundation; who knows how far you can go?

BEING OPEN TO CHANGE

In current human nature there still seems to be a strong need to belong and feel we are a part of something rather than a unit in isolation. The fact is we are a part of something much bigger than ourselves; we are part of the human race. This is the group we should belong to and this alone should be enough to feel a sense of unity.

Regrettably, most of us do not feel like this within, so we look outwardly for something with which to identify ourselves: religions, cults, nationality, sports and fashion, etc. Often it seems that if we do not belong to something external, we feel isolated and lost, as if we are not alive. Once again, all we need to do is to tune in to the human path of evolution and we will find fulfilment. We will know that we belong to something special because it is a real inner feeling, not an intellectual choice. The moment we experience this all the external desires of belonging will seem irrelevant and artificial.

There is one particular misconception it is essential to clarify and correct, if we want to move forward in the path of evolution.

We do not need food in order to have the energy to do things,

we do not need to receive in order to give,

we do not need to be loved in order to give love and so on;

we already have everything we need,

it is all upside down.

The first thing we do in the moment of birth is breathe in.

We receive energy and life from that moment forward. After the childhood phase, the emphasis has to shift to giving. Do not think that you need to eat in order to have energy. Do whatever you have to do; using the energy you have inside, until you feel the need for food. The giving and utilization comes first; the act of replenishing the energy you have consumed will follow naturally.

Do not expect anything. Give to others your time and energy and you will receive the same as a natural consequence. Love unconditionally; you do not need to be loved in order to love. Inside of all of us is enough love to brighten any dark corner of the world; give love and love will come back to you as a consequence.

But, and *this is important*, it will only happen if you mean it.

How can we mean it if our present level of consciousness is

limited, as well as our capacity for being unselfish? Simply start small, make sure your actions are real and build on them. If you honestly discover you are unable to give without having first received, do not force it, just focus on taking care of your body and mind. Rest assured it will happen in time, and when it does you will never look back.

Please understand there is no need to hang on to belief systems in order to feel fulfilled. We often have the psychological need to hang on to old belief systems, or traditions, because they give us security and a sense of belonging. In order to fulfil our potential we must be open to change, which can happen at any time. Change starts with a continuous inner growing that occasionally manifests as external changes of personal behaviour. For this to happen successfully it will be necessary to let go of old ineffective models in order to embrace the new.

Change can be scary but there is nothing to fear, because inside each one of us are all the resources we need to be able to cope with change. It is a part of our makeup as human beings to have an amazing ability to evolve, step by step, into something extraordinary. So do not worry, we cannot go faster than our present level of evolution will allow us; whatever happens, you have the inner capacity to deal with it.

REACHING THE CENTRE OF THE UNIVERSE

'To be the centre of the universe'. We often hear this phrase when someone wants to be the centre of attention. Others seem to be constantly searching for the centre of the universe; where the action is really happening. Sometimes, we also believe a person is the centre of the universe so we try to get close to them.

Places like Los Angeles, New York and London seem to be the centre of the universe; the places where things are happening, where the future is being written. The centre of the universe can even be a fabulous party, in some celebrity villa, or at a Hollywood film premiere.

Some people continuously look for places and events where, at least for a while, the centre of the universe seems to be located. The quest for success and fame are also ways to get to the centre of the universe; to be a part of the 'elite' perceived as creating trends and making their mark on our society.

Some desperately try to get there and when it does not happen (as in most cases), they feel rejected. They feel they are failures and mourn 'what could have been' reluctantly carrying on, while feeling they have missed something vital.

The select few who have managed to achieve the fame and notoriety for which they craved believe, for a while, they are close to the centre of the universe; until they realise, they are still not there, yet. It seems there is always another place, another situation, another party or another group of people who are really the centre of the universe.

This centre of the universe is quite elusive. It always seems to be somewhere else, with some other group, with some other trend, at some other location. The truth is, if we look for the centre of the universe outside ourselves, we will never find it. It becomes a mad search taking us on a long, fruitless, journey. The place we really need to be is right where we are now, at this moment. The time is always now. Understand there is no need to wait and hope that maybe one day... [Fill in the blank]. *That day is today, now and always.*

Right now you may not feel you are the centre of the universe and that is understandable; the reality is quite the opposite. Do not worry whether you will be the centre of the universe soon, because the centre is everywhere there is harmony and in everyone that is in tune.

It does take time to get in tune, but not as long as we may think, when we know what to do. It is easier when we are young, because our minds are not yet overloaded with past memories; we are fresh and full of energy and positivity. As we get older we have to work a bit harder in the beginning, but after some time the knowledge and experience we acquired during our life will become an invaluable asset.

To get in tune is the most important thing we can do with our time. Indeed, at the moment, the meaning of life is to get in tune and carry on the process of evolution (a meaning that will take different forms as we evolve), everything else is just a red herring; one of the many roads leading to nowhere.

It is true that sometimes we need to travel many roads leading nowhere, just to realise you still are...nowhere. We have done that for quite some time now and a change is necessary. We have to be in awareness in order to take a journey that leads to somewhere; and an amazing journey it will be.

In the meantime, you have to be patient for a little while longer. Begin the process of inner connection and soon the centre of the universe will be a real experience, not an illusionary fantasy.

The Path of Evolution

If you are a person belonging to an organized religious group, a believer in a God and his plan for humanity, you may feel you are already in the right path; everyone else belonging to other religious groups is not. Some have quite rigid views while others believe all paths are leading to God.

Either way, if that is what you believe, it is fine with me. Personally, I believe there is only one path; the path of evolution and, as explained throughout this book, you need to take certain steps to get on it. It is quite easy to realise when you are on it because what you feel and experience is real. It is not a concept, not a belief system, not an intellectual idea...it is real.

You will feel truly connected to everyone and everything; you will not have a single negative thought, word or action; you will envy no one, be angry or resentful with anyone.

When you wake up in the morning, you will not consider yourself as a separate unit, thinking of ways to achieve your individual happiness. Instead, your thoughts will be towards common good, how to create harmony and the ability to apply the ancient model of 'Good Thoughts, Good Words, Good Deeds'. It bears repeating again and again, *it is easier than you may think.*

If you belong to a religious group and you are living the reality I have just described, continue doing what you are doing. If you are not, be honest with yourself and do not be afraid of change because it is the beginning of something much bigger.

If you are starting to get fed up with my 'getting in tune' mantra, I'm sorry, but it is the only way I know to fully experience the human essence. Still, do not spend too much time analysing intellectually, just do it. If it makes sense to you, do not waste any more time, it will be a real experience not a hypothesis or belief system. Your body, mind and senses (and eventually some extra ones) will tell you so.

We are all equally important, regardless of race, religion or social status because in all of us there is the capacity to tune in into the path of evolution. You will need no money, power, fame or anything similar; everything you need is inside of you.

Forget about the experts who try to make you feel ignorant and dependent. When it comes to your body and mind, you are the only expert. You could be the person helping all of us to move forward; you could discover some inner potentialities that are still a mystery. Regardless of your present condition do not feel powerless; you are not. No one in the world is in a better position than you; you are the scientist.

You may feel yourself to be behind in the journey but time is irrelevant. You could achieve in a moment what someone else may have done in a year or more... nothing is impossible.

You are free because you are a human being with all the resources you need within you. Soon you will be free of dogmas, crippling past belief systems, rigid points of views and free of chemicals poisoning your body and mind as you move towards the next stage of evolution.

CHAPTER TWELVE

LIVING IN THE LIGHT

BECOMING AN ALCHEMIST

Our minds and bodies are our laboratories of discovery and we are destroying this amazing gift with excess chemicals and medicines. The natural progression in our human journey can only happen with awareness; inner focus is the way forward, so it is paramount that we stay in the path.

Because they are not in harmony with our bodies and mind, drugs and medicine should only be used when absolutely necessary. Sometimes we will have no choice but to take them, but try your best not to reach that point; practise prevention.

Often I see people doing different types of physical activity, in order to 'let off steam', such as tension, stress, anger and frustration. These activities can take many forms such as boxing, running, aerobic exercises or pretty much anything that make us sweat and feel relieved at the end. Where does all the 'steam' go? Whatever type of energy you expend from your body, it has to go somewhere; nothing disappears. Therefore, any negative energy released into the environment only contributes to the negativity or 'evil' we experience in the world.

We should really become more aware of what creates the negative energy in our bodies and mind, and try to avoid those factors. If that is not possible, we should transform the negative energies into positive ones, before releasing them into the environment; this is what true alchemy is all about. This is what it means to transmute something 'base' into 'gold'.

To turn the tide we have to become alchemists. Furthermore, we must, consciously, absorb negativity from the environment and, through the alchemic process, change it into positivity before releasing it. Essentially, we have to become cleaners. Whenever we are in a negative environment we have to try our best to create harmony; as a sensitive, aware, human being you will absorb that negativity and evil from the environment.

Find some time, sit quietly, and change the negative energy you have absorbed from the environment into a positive energy. Breathe, relax, connect with your Higher Self, and see the negativity that you have absorbed for what it is; a darkness created by the absence of the light of consciousness.

Now fill your being with this light, until there is not even a tiny space inside you that is not filled by it, then release it into space.

MEDITATION

Meditation has nothing to do with religion. People seem reluctant to meditate because they believe it is a religious practice but it is not. Lately, the word meditation has been used quite liberally. Under its umbrella many teach relaxation or visualization techniques, while others focus on breathing exercises, chanting, mantras, and so on. I want to clarify what meditation is and the reasons for doing it. To do so, we must talk about our personalities.

We are all born with certain characteristics within us. This 'essence' makes us unique, what others may call our 'soul' or 'spirit'. Who we believe we are, is our personality (or persona), but this is just the superficial expression of our essence.

Our personality is just the result of the times and place we were born, our social and family background, our past experiences and our perceptions of life and reality. Born in a different time and place, we would still have the same 'essence', but it would manifest itself differently.

In simpler terms, if you were born in a suburb of England, to a middle class family with specific religious and social views, you would tend to develop certain characteristics. Your personal experiences would add to that and you would develop a certain way of talking, thinking with an overall perception of life.

If, instead, you were born in India, with a different religious and social background, apart from the obvious difference in skin colour, you would develop a very different type of personality; the way you talk, think, your perception of life, your background and experiences would have combined to create a personality very different from the English persona.

At the core of your being you are the same, in either scenario, but your essence (soul, spirit, etc.) would manifest itself differently, according to the place, time and background of your upbringing.

What we *really are* is...the essence.

What we *believe* we are is just the personality created by various circumstances and beliefs.

How can we connect with our essence to find out who we *truly are*, regardless of the circumstances that created our personalities? *That is the purpose of meditation.*

Our minds are our personality. Throughout our lives we use our mind to analyse and understand our environment. We formulate opinions, beliefs and ways to interact with others upon the type of information and experiences we absorb. Our thoughts are always connected with our personality, because they have created it in the first place. The mind is the personality; one cannot exist without the other; which is why we can only connect with our essence when the mind is still.

By that I mean the absence of thoughts and complete stillness. Through constant practise, we have to slow down the thought process (which keeps us living in the personality) to the point where we can achieve complete stillness of the mind.

In that moment there are no thoughts, nothing.

It also means that, in that moment, we cease to exist.

Who we believe we are — our personality — is gone; no more John, Mary, Abdul, Patel, Lee, Brigitte or Francesca. This momentary death of our personalities allows us to experience and connect to our essence.

Even if for only a few seconds, it will change our lives.

To evolve it is vital that we connect with our essence. By doing this we achieve complete awareness (relative to our current stage of evolution). This will guide us and keep us on the right path to achieving complete fulfilment of our human nature.

The fact that we are not connected to, or even aware of, our essence comes from our still primitive level of evolution. It should not surprise us; we are still larvae, not butterflies. In order to become such, we have to embrace real spirituality and connect with our essence. This will result in an amazing discovery; all of our essences are unique, yet the same. At the core we are one. When this happens, all of the hate, divisions, wars, and similar nonsense will cease because they can only exist in the cocoon of the personality, not as a butterfly of essence. *This is the purpose of meditation.* I hope many of you will approach it with this intention in mind.

CONNECTING WITH THE ENVIRONMENT

Here is a technique that will help you better connect with the elements in our environment and inner qualities. With practice it will help you view the world through completely different eyes. It is also a wonderful exercise to teach your children; they will become more connected with their environment, rather than separated from it. As with all focus exercises make sure you have created a tranquil environment so you can relax completely.

You will have two different parts to this focus exercise; one in the morning and the other in the evening.

In the morning, focus on major elements.

Contemplate things like water, trees, flowers, grass, fruit, vegetables, grains, seeds etc.

For example, on Monday morning you focus on water. Once you are relaxed, begin to think about water, its meaning, its function on the planet. Think about rain,
the sea or the water in our bodies that we need to survive. What we are doing is connecting with the essence of water; understanding why water exists.

Do this for about three to five minutes.

Then on Tuesday maybe you focus on trees. What trees do for the planet, the carbon dioxide, etc. In fact, make it interesting by first doing a bit of research. And you continue to focus on a different element each morning.

We do this exercise to create a deeper connection with the element.

For example, every time you drink a glass of water, you will find the experience is different. You no longer drink it mechanically just to quench your thirst; you have connected with it, its meaning and its essence. Similarly when you walk past a tree and touch it, there is a different experience; it's a spiritual connection. *This is what real spirituality is. It is the reality of life and the awareness of how things are interconnected.*

In the evening, focus on inner qualities.

Such as love: focus on what love is, the impact of love on society and the world, the 'essence' of love; feel it, understand it, become familiar with it. On another evening do the same with other inner qualities like peace, kindness, harmony, justice, equality and so on. You are doing the same thing, as with with the major elements, by focusing on the deeper meaning of that quality.

The next time there is a situation where love, kindness, peace or any other inner quality on which you have previously focused is involved, you will have a very different connection to that quality which will, probably, produce different external actions.

I truly believe this is what we should teach our children to do at home and at school. Children have an amazing capacity to understand and 'connect' in this manner, because their minds are still so receptive and less judgmental.

LIGHT AND DARKNESS

I'd like you to remember, even in your darkest hour, there is no such thing as darkness, everything is light. In our present level of evolution we can only perceive a tiny spectrum of light, everything else that we are not able to see we call darkness...but there is no darkness.

The only darkness that exists is in our still primitive level of consciousness and capabilities. As we evolve further everything will be light and love, because this is the reality of the universe; everything else is an illusion, created by our limited senses. The only way to know that this is a reality, and not intellectual wishful thinking, is by tuning in. Beyond that, I can only remind you that you will not find the answer in your mind for the reasons you learned when discussing meditation.

If there are enough spiritual people on the planet we will be able to overcome any obstacle, and against the most daunting odds. If there are not enough spiritual people, then our future is very bleak. If you believe you are on the cusp, please think carefully about the consequences of your actions. In fact, there is no cusp, nothing is neutral and everything you do either serves darkness or light.

Become aware of the impact you can have on our future, every single person can make an incredible difference. No one is perfect but do be sure your scale is tilting more and more towards the light of real spirituality.

Staying Committed

I understand that not everyone is interested in many of the topics I have described in this book. For many of you the everyday routine of working and looking after a family takes pretty much all of your time. However, if what you have read make sense to you, start with the basics.

In the manner I have explained start taking care of your body and mind; we can all do that. Then you will begin to feel better and more in tune. Once this becomes regular practice, you will find yourself wanting to expand your knowledge and increase your awareness. Then when you established your inner

Chairman, you may discover it quite easy to find the space and time to follow the right path to the next stage of evolution.

The reality is we have a very short time to grow up, but it does not take very long when we are committed to the process, especially if there are many others committed as well. What slows us down are the conflicting opinions, the fear of being different and the idea if the majority does not do it, we must be wrong. To some degree those thoughts are understandable, that is why it is very important to associate with those of like minds. You must remember you are never alone and very soon you will know this as a certainty.

One of the central ideas we need to learn is to be kind to ourselves. We are not sinners, there is nothing fundamentally wrong with who we are. We are just children, with limited knowledge and understanding, so let's not judge ourselves too harshly because of our limitations. We have to love ourselves for what we are and do the same for others. The truly evolving are interested in harmony and unselfish love, so remember not to be angry with anyone who thinks and acts otherwise. Remember, those who are the creators of negativity, pain and suffering to others are very limited. They may believe they are clever and sometimes superior to others; they do not realise they still belong to the primordial level of human evolution. How funny that some of these people believe otherwise.

What is important for you is to stay committed by taking regular steps in the direction of true spirituality. In every generation many people are attracted towards the ideas of spirituality, consciousness and social change issues, but usually their commitment is short-lived.

Some practise Yoga, recite prayers or mantras, take active interests in world problems and believe they are the generation to create a fundamental change towards world peace and so on.

I have seen it few times with younger people when, after a few years, their youthful energy and optimism begins to wane. Gradually it is replaced by self-centred interests and the everyday responsibilities of family, the mortgage, career and so on. These issues pretty much absorb all their time and focus until we hear the phrase spoken so many times before, 'Oh my God,

I've become just like my parents!'

The reason all of these youthful fires and beliefs die out is due to one common thing: they lack a real foundation, they are just intellectual fantasies combined with wishful thinking. The actions being carried out during this phase is what's in vogue at the moment. Even the oldest practices, like Yoga and meditation, are approached superficially with little understanding and without the necessary support of a healthy body and clear mind as developed through this book.

IT IS NOT IMPORTANT WHAT YOU BELIEVE,

WHAT IS IMPORTANT IS THE ACTION YOU TAKE.

You may be Christian, Muslim, Jewish, Hindu, maybe you reject organized religions but believe there is an elite that is manipulating us towards an Orwellian one world dictatorship. Perhaps you believe we are controlled by extraterrestrial entities from another dimension, it really does not matter. Even if we do not agree on the causes of all the darkness, and rampant evil, on the planet, what is important is that we agree on the solution.

In this book, I have introduced what I believe to be the solution; we have to be healthy in body and mind, be connected with our Higher Self so our actions are motivated by the good of all, and be involved in every aspect of life, taking an immediate responsibility to create a harmonious future.

There is one thing you can do, the moment you finish reading this book, and that is to connect with the vast amounts of love, light and positivity within yourself; consciously send it to every particle of your being, reaching every aspect of your personality, and then send it to everyone...including those with personalities you may not be fond of! If you find this difficult to do, send it to their essence, and then it will be like sending it to yourself; at the core we are all one, so this benefits us all.

One thing is for certain, we cannot carry on as we are doing now, we have reached a dead end. I am confident we can change things for the better, and soon, but each one of us must take responsibility, immediately, because the change can only happen by developing conscious awareness.

In spite of present day religious and political leaders, big corporations and the über-rich, many of whom are spiritually unbalanced and motivated by the greedy and selfish aspects of their personalities; a harmonious future can still be a reality.

The human being of the future has to be a healthy individual motivated by principles and visions derived from the Higher Self. These future beings have to be the leaders and the guides, in every aspect of our lives, so we can create the ideal ground to further our process of evolution towards oneness and harmony.

If you agree do not hesitate, act immediately and commit to the process. A new vibration is coming through, resonating in the hearts of those who are moving towards a state of conscious awareness. We must turn on our inner light, tune in to this higher vibration and come together as ONE.

I sincerely hope this book helps you.

Daniele

MY FRIEND (PART TWO)

My friend smiled...'Are you happy with your book?'

'Yes' I replied, 'it is all I wanted to say for the moment'.

'Do you have any expectations?'

'Yes...I hope it will resonate with people. This book is just the starting point, there is so much more that needs to be said and shared. And, if there is enough interest, I will write another one where I can go further...much further'.

My friend became serious, 'So you still have expectations? I thought you would have learned by now'.

'Well' I said, 'it is ok for me to have expectations because you do not'.

My friend laughed. 'Have you managed to stay away from the mystical nonsense?'

'Oh yes' I replied, 'absolutely'.

My friend smiled... and then he disappeared.

The Last Word

If you enjoyed this book and believe in its contents, please talk about it and share it with your family and friends. As mentioned throughout this introductory book, in order to create change we must have pure and unselfish intentions so it is very important for like-minded people to connect worldwide. Therefore, I am prepared to attend public conferences, seminars and workshops whenever there is a genuine demand.

Please visit my website, *www.meetdaniele.com* or email me at *daniele@meetdaniele.com*

ABOUT THE AUTHOR

Daniele has dedicated his life studying, practising, teaching and researching various methods and traditions in order to discover the true spiritual path. From Persia to India, China to Japan; from the Tibetan temples, to the mystery schools of Egypt and Greece, Essenes to Alchemy; this natural progression has led him to modern disciplines with the study of Psychoanalysis, Hypnosis and thence to N.L.P. and other evolving techniques.

Today, the core of his highly effective methods is based on the understanding and knowledge of human nature.

Lightning Source UK Ltd.
Milton Keynes UK
UKOW051008060812

197115UK00001B/4/P